Gangbangers

Much love to my wife, Donna, and my kids, Carrie, Dan, Amy, and Kelly, who must tolerate my preoccupation with my writing projects.

Loren Christensen

Gangbangers

Understanding the Deadly Minds of America's Street Gangs

Paladin Press • Boulder, Colorado

Also by Loren W. Christensen:

Anything Goes
Deadly Force Encounters (with Alexis Artwohl)
Extreme Joint Locking
Far Beyond Defensive Tactics
Fighting Dirty (video)
Master and Styles (with Mark Hatmaker and Vince Morris)
Restraint and Control Strategies (video)
Skid Row Beat
Speed Training
Speed Training: The Video
Surviving Workplace Violence
Vital Targets (video)
Warriors: On Living with Courage, Discipline, and Honor
The Way Alone

Gangbangers:
Understanding the Deadly Minds of America's Street Gangs
by Loren W. Christensen

ISBN 10: 1-58160-047-X
ISBN 13: 978-1-58160-047-6

Printed in the United States of America

Published by Paladin Press, a division of
Paladin Enterprises, Inc.,
Gunbarrel Tech Center
7077 Winchester Circle
Boulder, Colorado 80301 USA
+1.303.443.7250

Direct inquiries and/or orders to the above address.

TABLE OF CONTENTS

"Too many people will not testify about gang crimes because they are afraid of violent reprisal. We must not allow the voice of justice to be frightened into silence by the violent threats of gangs . . . I am determined to break the backs of criminal gangs that have ruined too many lives and stolen too many futures by bringing the full force of the law against them."

—President Bill Clinton

ACKNOWLEDGMENTS

This book would have been impossible to write without the help of many people on both sides of the gang issue from around the country who so generously shared their knowledge and experience. In addition to those listed below, there were other people who helped but for whatever reason wanted to remain anonymous.

- Detective Stu Winn, Portland, Oregon, Police Bureau's Gang Enforcement Team
- Jesse Beckom Jr., author of *Gangs, Drugs, & Violence Chicago Style*
- Sgt. Bill Valentine, Corrections, Nevada State Prisons (retired)
- Officer Scott Gammon, Fort Collins, Colorado, Police Services Gang Intervention Unit
- Supervisor John L. Miller, Department of Juvenile and Adult Community Justice, Portland, Oregon
- Program Administrator Jimmy Brown, Department of Juvenile and Adult Community Justice, Portland, Oregon

- Erika Sylvester, Adult Parole and Probation, Multnomah County, Oregon, Gang Supervision Unit
- Steve Nawojczyk, Pulaski County Coroner, Little Rock, Arkansas (retired)
- Supervisor Tim Clemmens, Yakima County Juvenile Detention, Yakima, Washington
- Sandra Davis, ex-gangbanger, now operating Mothers Against Gang Wars, Los Angeles, California
- Albert, Hispanic ex-gangbanger, a city on the West Coast
- "Angel," Hispanic gangbanger, a city in Arkansas
- Joseph Marshall Jr., cofounder of San Francisco's Omega Boys Club, California
- Pamela Sowers, writer and gang observer
- Detective Jack Simington, Kennewick Police Department, Kennewick, Washington
- Officer Mike Stradley, Portland (Oregon) Police Bureau, Gang Enforcement Team
- Louie Lira, Hispanic ex-gangbanger, now a gang specialist with the Youth Gang Program in Portland, Oregon
- Detective Doug Justice, Portland (Oregon) Police Bureau
- Bill Ottaway, ex-racist skinhead
- "Hellraiser," ex-gangbanger

AUTHOR'S NOTE

A GANG IS A GROUP OF PEOPLE WHO

- interact among themselves to the exclusion of other groups;
- have a group name, a common identifying sign or symbol, or an identifiable leadership;
- claim a neighborhood or territory;
- create a climate of fear and intimidation within the community;
- communicate in a peculiar or unique style;
- wear distinctive types of clothing or exhibit distinctive appearance; and
- engage in criminal or antisocial behavior on a regular basis.

WARNING SIGNS FOR GANG ACTIVITY INCLUDE

- gang graffiti or drawings on notebooks, clothing, skin, or walls;
- sudden aggressive behavior;
- alienation;

- new friends who appear antisocial or ganglike;
- favorable attitude toward gangs and drugs;
- wearing of specific colors or gang attire;
- gang tattoos;
- residency in a neighborhood where there are gangs;
- dislike for authority: parents, teachers, police;
- lack of hobbies or interests;
- decline in grades;
- truancy;
- new conflicts with parents;
- use of hand signs and gang verbiage; and
- new use of drugs and alcohol.

INTRODUCTION

Gangs ain't going away quickly. No matter how many have members killed by their own peers, no matter how many the police put into jail, no matter how many government bucks are given to feel-good organizations to reach out and interface with them—gangs and gangbangers keep increasing like cockroaches in a shabby tenement. And gangs are getting nastier, too. Ten years ago, they fought with fists, clubs, and pistols. Now they use an array of sophisticated weapons.

"I had a shooting recently, and I had never before seen the type of bullet used," one veteran gang detective told me. "I had to take it to a gun expert to see what kind of new round it was. Gangs have some incredible firepower now, they have lots of it, and they don't think twice about using it."

Gangs are no longer a big-city problem. They are everywhere now: the suburbs, rural areas, and small-town America. They have become so common in the big cities that gang shootings hardly make the five o'clock news anymore. In my city, Portland, Oregon, news programs led with gang stories all through the late 1980s and into the early '90s. Not now, and it's not because the problem has gone away. In fact, it's worse now than ever, but gang crimes, such as drive-by shootings, are mundane today. People are either apathetic or desensitized to them; they want to see something else on the news. To get press these days, there has to be a real twist or novelty to a gang killing, say an innocent person getting caught in the crossfire or a shoot-out on a school playground.

The following example of such a twist happened recently in Portland. A man and his wife walked out of a downtown theater and decided to take a stroll along the waterfront since it was beautiful summer evening. Five blocks away, two rival gangs fired at each other, and a second later, the man, a father of four, fell dead at his wife's feet. What happened? One of the gangbanger's stray bullets had traveled five blocks and across four busy intersections before hitting the innocent victim, who had been standing on the corner waiting for the traffic signal to change.

This shooting was splashed all over the news for several days. It was a scary story because the victim was simply in the wrong place at the wrong time. It struck home with people, since the man could have been any of the hundreds of thousands of people watching the news and reading the newspaper. It was an oddity in the news biz, but was it the only shooting that happened that week? No way. In fact, there were many others, but they were just the run-of-the mill kind: gangbanger versus gangbanger clashing in the littered streets of gang-infested neighborhoods. (As I'm completing the last rewrite on this book, I learned that the gangbanger who fired the fatal round pled guilty and was sentenced to 23 years. Let's hope he has a miserable experience in prison.)

My point is that if you are no longer hearing about gang warfare where you are, especially if you live in a medium to large city, don't kick back and think that it's gone away. More than likely it's just not newsworthy anymore.

So, what the heck is going on? Why haven't we been able to make a dent in the proliferation of street gangs? The police have definitely gotten better at working them, our prisons have become expert at incarcerating them, parole and probation officers work hard making them fulfill their obligations, and community groups do all they can to get young people out of the gang life. But still the gangs rage, and hundreds of young lives bleed out on our streets every year. One gang detective told me the reason he decided to transfer to another job in his agency was that "I just got real tired of seeing dead kids in the street."

We have got to do something because, as they say in corny movies, "people are dying." Of course, there are always those people who say, "Hey, they're just killing each other, so let 'em. In fact, let's put them all in a big stadium, give them all the guns and ammo they want, and let 'em go at it. We'll just wait outside and pretend we're listening to a popcorn bag in the microwave. When we hear the last pop, we'll know it's over."

Well, until this happens, gangbangers will continue to redden the streets, not only with their own blood but with that of the innocent. People in the wrong place at the wrong time, like the husband and father of four above. Other examples from my city are the old Vietnamese man, who was holding his infant grandson while sleeping in bed, when a shower of drive-by bullets punched through the wall and exploded his head like a dropped melon, and the little girl who was playing on her porch when a stray round fired by a gangbanger tore into her tiny body.

When I began to compile information for this project and would mention to people that I was working on a book about how gangbangers think, I heard repeatedly: "That should be a pretty short book. They don't think at all, do they?" At first blush, especially when we read about the senselessness of some of their actions, that may indeed seem to be the case. But those of us who have worked with gangs and continue to work with them and those young people who have gotten out of the life or are still in the thick of it know that they do think.

They think about drugs, revenge, and respect. They think a lot about their reputation and how they can enhance it. They think about going to prison and about surviving once they are there. They think about making babies and raising them in the gang life. They think about how to avoid the police and how to fight them when they can't. They think about their parole and probation officers who force them to do what they don't want to do. And they think about killing people and about getting killed themselves.

I talked to a lot of people to make this book happen—current gangbangers and ex-gangbangers, gang cops, prison corrections officers, parole and probation officers, juvenile counselors—people who know a lot about how gangbangers' minds work. What I found early in the project, after I'd conducted only a few interviews, was that the bangers and the experts were writing the book for me (though I got stuck with the typing). Their opinions, experiences, threats, accusations, and fears revealed exactly how gangbangers think. Since their voices said it more dramatically and chillingly than I ever could, I let them talk with as little intrusion from me as possible.

If this book frightens you, don't feel alone. Although I worked with gangs for several years as a police officer, what I learned while working on this project scared the hell out of me. Gangbangers are angrier now, they hate more, they're less hesitant to use firepower, they're less intimidated by the police and of going to prison, and many of them have mentally accepted the probability of their early, violent death.

What can we do about it? I haven't the foggiest idea, and it seems no one else does either. We've incarcerated the gangbangers, but most of them come out of the joint worse than they were when they went in. We've love-bombed them with hugs, compassion, and Big Brother programs, but as you will see, many of them just laugh at those efforts. We've run them out of town, but they are quickly replaced by others who are just like them. It's like trying to drain the ocean with a cup.

What I observed while working in the gang unit and with the police bureau in general is that far too many times the experts on an issue are not consulted. Instead, programs are created and units are formed by people who "think" they have a solution.

Well, I went to the experts—people who work with gang-bangers for a living—and asked them to tell me what they see going on in the minds of those kids to whom violence comes so easily. And I talked with people who bang in the 'hood every day, asking them to look deep into their minds to see how they feel about a variety of issues.

This book is the result of those conversations. This is how gangbangers think.

CHAPTER 1

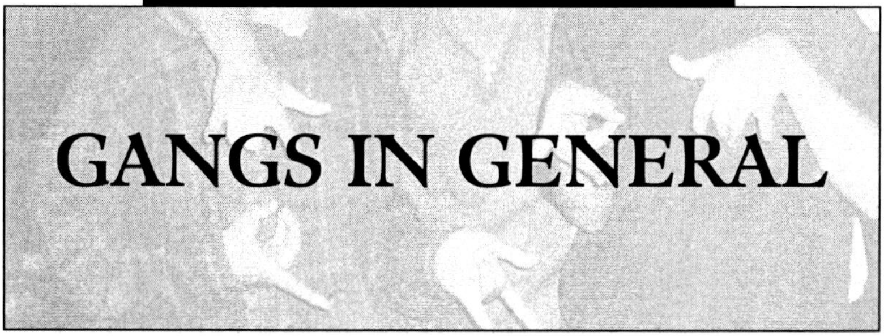

GANGS IN GENERAL

"All the children are insane."

—The Doors

I did a lot of theater in college and learned to appreciate musicals and theatrical dancing, which there is plenty of in *West Side Story*. It's a Romeo and Juliet tale of the love of a white guy from one street gang for a Puerto Rican girl whose brother belongs to a rival street gang. Of course, this causes conflict, as it does in today's gang culture, but the difference is that in the musical/movie the characters dance and sing about the dilemma. Nonetheless, a couple of the gangbanger/dancer/singers die from a very choreographed dance/fight in which knives and zip guns are used. Although the movie is decades old now, it still holds up. It portrays gang rivalry, turf battles, weapons play, racism, wanna-bes, loyalty to the gang, cops, and senseless death. Sound familiar?

Although the movie does end tragically, overall there is a sense of innocence to it relative to what is happening in today's bloody streets. In the movie, the fights are choreographed to capture the art of dance, and there is a sense of drama, humor, fun. The 1950s language sounds odd, and the weapons used in the battles are mostly chains, clubs, knives, and homemade zip guns. Music and dancing aside, *West Side Story* does a good job of conveying a sense of what gangs were about back in the old days.

Oh how far we have come. Today, gangs are part of virtually every community, large and small; indeed they have become part of our culture. Gang culture has permeated movies, television shows, music videos, clothing styles, language, art, and other areas of our everyday life. Its ugliness is now mainstream.

Unlike the ones depicted in *West Side Story,* today's gangs kill at the smallest provocation. The wrong facial expression (getting "mean-mugged") by a rival gang member can spark a hail of gunfire. As an example, on one occasion I investigated a case at a local high school where a non-gang-involved Vietnamese student mean-mugged a Vietnamese gang member as he passed in the hallway. Offended, the gangbanger walked two blocks to an Asian grocery store, bought a meat cleaver, returned to the school, and hacked it into the shoulder of the kid who mean-mugged him, nearly slicing all the way through. The gangbanger then walked back to the store, told the proprietor that he didn't need the cleaver (he cleaned it before returning it), and got his money back. All this over the wrong facial expression.

As I was working on this book, three gangsters in Tacoma, Washington, a couple hours from where I sit, barged into a Vietnamese restaurant and sprayed the place with gunfire. When the pandemonium ended, five people were dead and five others were wounded. At this writing, the motive appears to be revenge over a past incident involving a stolen purse from a car parked behind the restaurant.

There have been other incidents; in fact, there were a half-dozen gang-related deaths around the Portland area during the four months I spent on this project. Indeed, violent death comes easy to today's gangbangers.

In *West Side Story,* the kids carried chains and clubs. Now, gang members are armed with .40-calibers, 9mms, automatics, pipe bombs, hand grenades, and in one case napalm. In the movie, the street gangs targeted one person, but today's gangs are willing to hit innocent bystanders as they "overkill" their target. It's quite common for dozens of rounds to be sprayed at a group of people on a street corner, in a club, and at a home, in hopes that one or more of the rounds will find its target. Sometimes the target gets hit, but more times than not others fall, too.

People smoked reefer (marijuana) during the era of *West Side Story.* Today, drugs are one of the driving forces behind many gangs; the wheeling and dealing of them have caused multitudes of deaths over the years. Gangbangers live in a fantasy where they see themselves living a lifestyle of great wealth, complete with fancy cars and clothes, desirable women, and power. Few of them make it, but scores of them die trying to get there.

In the movie, walls displayed graffiti of gang names and love proclamations. Tattoos in that era were of the same things they marked on walls, as well as the occasional dagger and naked hula dancer. Today, marking walls, tattooing, and signing with the hands have become a sophisticated and complex method of communication among gangbangers, and there have been many books and videos published to decipher their meanings. It's commonplace now for someone to be killed or seriously injured when a gangbanger is in the wrong place, displaying the wrong symbol. For example, a young man waiting for a bus in a Midwestern city reached for a pencil in his pocket and inadvertently pulled out a black bandana. When the bandana, which was the color worn by a local gang, fell to the sidewalk, two gang members wearing red approached. One of them, with a red bandana over his face said threateningly, "What's up, Blood? What's up with that rag?" He then retrieved a gun from his waistband and said, "Whatever, Blood," and pulled the trigger. When the boy with the black bandana fell, the shooter fired a second shot into his body, killing him over nothing more than the color of a piece of cloth.

Respect was important in the era of *West Side Story*, but the difference today is that countless lives end violently in retaliation over being "dissed," a slang word meaning that the person has been disrespected in some fashion. Not only does violence over this happen frequently on the street, but in prison no show of disrespect can go unchallenged. Retribution is essential; otherwise the prison gang member loses face and becomes a victim of other predators. To Southeast Asian gangbangers the concept of revenge holds great significance. Some say they will always seek revenge against a person who has wronged them, even it takes a hundred years (more on this in Chapter 6).

WHAT'S UP TODAY?

West Side Story was then, and now is now. As we move into the new millennium, gangs have been entrenched for several years, and, according to many experts, they are growing in number and becoming an even greater threat to the fabric of our society. According to recent statistics, there are more than 16,000 gangs active in this country, with at least half a million members who are responsible for more than 600,000 crimes every year.

I'm going to go out on a limb here and say that these numbers are probably far below what is true because of the restrictions on the way police agencies have to count. I know from working intelligence in Portland's Gang Enforcement Team that we were under strict guidelines as to how to document a gang member. In my case, I worked skinheads, and

Female gangbanger flashes a gang sign.

there were dozen of times when I knew a person was a skinhead, racist, or antiracist, but I couldn't label him or her as such in the police computer since the individual didn't fulfill all the legal criteria that were needed. The end result is that these people go uncounted. Additionally, different law enforcement agencies employ different methods to count gangs and gang members. There is also the matter of those organizations getting government funding for their efforts to help gang-affected youth. Many in law enforcement say that such organizations have a tendency to inflate the numbers to make the problem seem worse than it is (if that's even possible). So, in other words, the numbers may be larger (my opinion), or they may be smaller. For sure, there are hundreds upon hundreds of gangs, and thousands upon thousands of gang members. And both are increasing.

GANG CULTURE

The most logical way to get an understanding of the mentality of gangbangers is to look at the culture, their behavior, and their activities. To be a banger, one must act differently than other people who are not. The way they act not only separates them and underscores their gang identity, it also adds a degree of mystery and glamor to the minds of those people who are impressionable—in particular, other young people who are approaching gang age and thinking about it for themselves.

We must keep in mind that most gangbangers are in their teens. "Gangbangers' ability to think is somewhat limited," says Timothy Clemmens, detention supervisor at the Yakima County Juvenile Detention in Washington state. "Most are young, inexperienced, and have limited education. In addition, they must deal with all the physical changes and financial and social problems of being a teenager. Teens feel a need to be accepted. Sometimes the only ones to accept them are those in a gang."

To add mystery, glamor, and distinctiveness, gangs wear a certain type of attire and cover themselves with tattoos that identify their gang, their allegiance to it, and their philosophy. They stand and walk in a unique way; they posture and gesture and communicate in a way that separates them from others. They hold certain beliefs and have ways of thinking that are distinctive to their gang membership.

There are four basic terms used to describe a gangbanger's involvement. First, there is the *wanna-be,* a young person on the edge of being a gangbanger. I think the term ought to be changed to *gonna-be,* because, as we will discuss later, these kids are often extremely dangerous, sometimes more so than regular members. Next, there is the *peripheral* or *fence straddler*, a young person who hangs around a gang and may or may not participate in gang activity. An *affiliate* is the person we usually think of when we think of a gangbanger. He has been accepted in the gang and participates in gang activity on a regular basis. The last term is *hard-core*, a person who lives totally for the gang, often referred to in gang vernacular as "down for the hood." He will do anything—kill or be killed for his precious gang.

Most young people go through an evolutionary mental and physical process, beginning with the gonna-be stage and progressing all the way to hard-core. As they begin moving down the path, they engage in minor gang activity, such as flashing hand signs, marking their territory, hanging around with other bangers, and so on. As they mature into the gang culture, developing knowledge, confidence, and status, their activities escalate to assaults, drug dealing, drive-by shootings, and homicide. With some, this progression may take a matter of a few weeks; for others, it may take longer, maybe even a year or so. Some may not make it at all as a result of something happening in their lives along the way, such as someone intervening and turning them around. A few might move away from the temptation, while others are jailed or killed before they get too far along the path.

"THE THREE R'S"

Let's move into an area that might be called "the three R's," and I'm not talking about reading, 'riting, and 'rithmetic. I'm referring to three elements that are of utmost importance to gangbangers' mentality as well as the reasons why most gangs form as a unit in the first place. The three R's—respect, reputation, and revenge—are paramount to gang culture, so much so that everyone I interviewed agreed that they are what being a gangbanger is all about, and what so many of them have died for.

Let's take a brief and generalized look at the three R's and also all the other elements so paramount to being a gangbanger. Later in the book we will look at these elements in more detail as they relate to each ethnic gang.

Respect

"People get into gangs because they think it's cool or because they want to impress somebody."

—a black gangbanger

"My role in my gang is to simply have respect from all and to let them know what's up with my set."

—a Hispanic gangbanger

"I have seen homeboys and rivals go down over turfs and colors and respect."

—a black gangbanger

"I joined a gang when I was 13. At first, being in a set meant that I was a part of something, and I thought I was someone."

—a female Hispanic gangbanger

"I see people walkin' around wearing their bandanas. I think they are cool; man, nobody would even think of messing with them. They have respect from other people."

—a gonna-be white gangbanger

"I'm from Stockton, California, where the real shit be going on and can't nobody fuck with us Laos, hoe. This is [gang name deleted] gang for life, hoe, so respect me when you see me, hoe."

—a Laotian gangbanger

"Respect my shit, and I'll respect y'all shit!"

—a black gangbanger

"Respect my shit and I'll respect ya'll shit."

We all want respect, which is to say that we want to be deserving of high regard. But gangbangers want it tenfold, not only for themselves but also for their gang, their family, their graffiti, their clothing and other symbols, and the turf they claim as their own. As we've already seen, a wrong look from a rival gang member or even a nongang member is looked upon as disrespect and can result in violence, even death. Sometimes a look can happen when the occupants of one car, who may not even be gang involved, give a hard look to the occupants of another car who are. John Miller, supervisor of Gang Resistance Intervention Team (GRIT), in Portland, Oregon, says, "We have seen a lot of road rage happen when a gang feels they have been dissed by people in a car. A mean mug is all it takes, and the guns come out."

In many gangs, it's required that members show disrespect to rival gangs—disrespect in the form of graffiti, assaults, hand signs, stare-downs, drive-bys, verbal challenges, and so on. If a member fails to diss a rival gang or gang member or fails to seek out revenge for being dissed, he is likely to be criticized or even beaten by his fellow gangbangers.

Reputation

"Soft niggas crumble when gangs come to the set. See, when I come to a nigga's set, niggas' hearts jump."

—a black gangbanger

Reputation, or rep, is critical to a gang member and the entire gang. Among racist skinheads, for example, there is enormous pride in saying that you are a white-power skinhead, meaning you are racist and possibly a Nazi. The skinhead member claims this title to anyone who will listen, because he knows that it strikes fear in the hearts of some people as a result of past horrific crimes committed by boot-stomping racist skinheads.

Whether the gangbanger is a Blood, Crip, Hammerskin, Viet Boy, or 18th Street, rep is all-important because it's one of the reasons the young person joined the gang in the first place. So important is it that it's quite common for a gangbanger to exaggerate his deeds in an attempt to get more of what is called "juice" in some gangs. The more juice a person has—the result of having a good rep—the more respect he gets and the higher his status. It's not uncommon for gangbangers to brag to the police about their rep and all that they have done to earn it, even admitting their involvement in crimes.

"Reputation is of the upmost importance to gangbangers," says Timothy Clemmens. "Many of them have been abused or neglected at home, and most have never been truly cared for. They do not want to be hurt or be forgotten again. When they see that the gang cares about them, they will do anything to please it. The gang is their parent and mentor, and they will emulate what they see other gang members doing. As they perform these same acts as the others, they build their reputation."

Revenge

"I know a lot of people that are from different sets, but I don't set-trip off them until someone set-trips off me."
—a white female gangbanger

Gang enforcement officers know that when there is a drive-by, a street brawl, or a disturbance in a school, there will be a retaliation. When a Blood kills a Crip or vice versa, officers step up their patrol in gang-infested areas and monitor the funeral in anticipation of a retaliatory shooting. It's rarely an issue of *Will it happen?* but rather *When will it happen?*

When a gangbanger holds the concept of revenge in high regard and, say, accidentally wanders into rival gang territory and gets confronted, challenged, or injured, he will naturally do everything in his power to make a hasty retreat. But in his mind the situation isn't over. He will definitely come back later to retaliate and save his and his gang's reputation.

Revenge happens because in gang thought, no challenge, assault, or diss goes unanswered. Remember, being a gang member is all about respect. So when disrespect occurs, swift revenge is exacted in an attempt to reestablish the rep. Revenge may be in the form of a bloody beating or a bullet-spray drive-by.

IDENTITY AND BELONGING

"I don't hang around those people [gangbangers] anymore. I still claim my turf for life, because I've always been taught by friends not to turn against my street and never turf-hop."
—a female black gangbanger

"I got much love to all my niggas on the block, strapped with Glocks."

—a black gangbanger

"My gang is my family. My homies are my blood."

—a black gangbanger

"My gang is my second family. All my homeboys are like my family. I trust them with my life, and they trust me with theirs. For years that's how it's been."

—a Hispanic gangbanger

"Gangs gave me the feeling of security and acceptance."

—a white ex-gangbanger

"It's a powerful feeling to know that there are guys willing to back you and die for you. It's a feeling that takes all the fear out of you."

—a skinhead gangbanger

"You have to stay true to the zoo."

—a white gangbanger

"Without gangs, no one would trip off the colors you wore."

—a black ex-gangbanger

Each gang prides itself on its identity and especially on its differences from other groups. Each member dresses, speaks, and marks graffiti in accordance with his or her particular gang. The members demonstrate the individuality of their gang as a way of showing pride as to where their hearts and minds are, disrespect to a rival gang, and camaraderie among their group. They often flash hand signs in the presence of the police, wear specific regalia to school, stand in a specific stance in court, and use gang-specific terminology no matter whom they are speaking with. After all, it's who they are, it's what they believe in, and, as has already been said and will be repeated often in the following pages, it's what some of them are willing to die for.

One of the major contributing factors to kids' getting into gangs is parental abuse and neglect. One time, my partner and I went to a house to try to catch a wanted gang member after an informant told us he was sleeping in a back room in his house. As we walked up on the porch, his sister told us that he was indeed in the back bedroom and that we could go on in the house.

We walked in as casual as can be, nodded to the mother, who was chatting on the phone and puffing on a cigarette, and then we went into the back bedroom and cuffed the kid before he could wake up. He had been shot in the leg the day before, so we weren't too worried about his leaping out the window. We then walked him (he hobbled) through the living room (where his mother was still talking and paying us no mind) and on out to the backseat of our car.

What is still amazing to me is that my partner and I were not in uniform; we were both wearing bluejeans and T-shirts. No one there told the mother who we were and what we were doing, nor did we, since she didn't look that interested, anyway. For all she knew, we could have been a couple of kidnappers walking into her house, snatching up her gangbanger kid, and walking out. She never asked us anything and never missed a beat talking on the phone. With a mother like that, no wonder the kid was all messed up. No wonder he needed to belong to a gang.

Many teens who join gangs have unstable family lives, where they feel unwanted or as though they don't fit in. As the kid searches for his identity, he often isolates himself and then seeks out others who are experiencing similar problems. When he is exposed to other people who are like him and there is no parent present to advise and guide him, the draw of the group can be a powerful one. In the gang, he will flourish because others are giving him the things his parents didn't. He is getting positive rewards and accepting his new role wholeheartedly. And once he is in, he is told over and over that there is no way out. This creates a sense of security and stability like he has never had before.

Gang members are devoted to their gang, and they often proclaim that they will back each other up and that they will fight to the death to defend their homies. From the outside they may appear angry, tough, and hostile, but there is a tenderness inside that allows them to form this bond that is based on need and a sort of love. Some experts say that it's a powerful emotion, one that goes beyond mere friendship. It's been my experience, however, that bangers give each other up in a heartbeat when the heat is on from the police or from their parole and probation officers.

Most gangs use an initiation process for new members, one that creates an almost instant sense of belonging to the new lifestyle and to the gangbangers who share it. The initiation is often violent: the new recruit is beaten by regular members, a process many gangs call "getting jumped in." Those who stand up to it feel a great sense of pride that they have survived. Then they feel even more pride as they are hugged after the ceremony by the very people who just beat them bloody.

Some gangs take the initiation a step farther and require the recruit to perform a crime, such as theft, gang rape, a drive-by, or a murder. One Hispanic gangbanger says that he knows of gangs that require a recruit to shoot his mother as an initiation and a way of showing willingness to do anything for the gang. This may be a fabrication, but who knows? The bottom line is that the initiation process is a sort of a rite of passage that instills in the new member a feeling of self-esteem and a sense of earning membership.

Joseph Marshall Jr., cofounder of San Francisco's Omega

Boys Club, an organization that combats the spread of gangs, says that all the elements that create this sense of belonging in a gangbanger's mind is based on skewed thinking. "Young people living in neighborhoods where guns seem more prevalent than books, where jobs are few and crack is king, surrounded by television, billboards, music, videos, and hustlers serving as role models, are duped into trusting what they see and hear. That is, to value materialism over the lives of others; to believe respect comes from peers, not from within; and to equate friendship with blind loyalty," he says.

THINKING IN THE NOW

Erika Sylvester, a parole and probation officer in the Gang Supervision Unit in Portland, Oregon, says that her gang clients think in terms of living from day to day. "It's all about how much money they can get today, not a year from now. It's about 'who's going to threaten me today?' They can't see five years down the road; some of them literally don't know the definition of the word *goal*. I've had to define it for them. With that philosophy, it's easy to see why so many act out with little thought given to the consequences of their actions."

It's common for gangbangers to say that they probably won't live to see the age of 25—and they don't even plan on it. You will see this mentioned in this book by people on both sides of the justice system. Of course, the "old" age of 25 may seem like a long time into the future to a 14-year-old kid, even one not involved in a high-risk lifestyle. But when you combine that outlook with the gang lifestyle that is filled with violence and death, 25 may indeed seem like an impossible goal to reach. With that mind-set, the alternative is to live in the now and to do whatever they please.

Living in the now makes some gangbangers fatalistic with their lives and the lives of others. It's demonstrated all the time as bangers casually pull out a gun in a public place and fire at a rival or a group of rivals. They stroll into restaurants and spray all who have the misfortune of choosing that moment to eat. There have been many times, though it still amazes the police, when gangsters have exchanged shots right in the presence of police officers. Sometimes, they even get out of their cars during traffic stops and point weapons at the police. For many bangers, doing that is the last thing they ever do.

"They live in a culture of guns and violence," says Portland Police Gang Detective Stu Winn. "Some don't think they have a future. They don't want to die, but they know it can happen at anytime."

MONEY

Gangbangers are criminals and, as such, they commit crimes to finance their activities. Selling drugs is seen as one of the biggest moneymakers, though few seem to be living a luxurious lifestyle. When times are good and there is a flow of cash, teenage gangbangers think they have it made because now they can get things—cars, jewelry, clothes—things that they once thought were symbols of success.

Joseph Marshall says, "Far too many people place material values first, even before human life. This is the price we pay when we teach our children that they must have material possessions in order to be OK. Our research at the Omega Boys Club, a violence prevention organization emphasizing academic achievement and noninvolvement with gangs or drugs, has shown us that the incidence of violent behavior/criminal activity increases as individuals embrace material values over human life."

For sure, some gangbangers are making a lot of money in the drug trade, as well as in gun sales, burglary, robbery, prostitution, and car theft. But there are a lot of other people making money off gangs, too, such as attorneys, judges, parole and probation officers, police officers, counselors, outreach people, and . . . ahem, writers. Indeed, if the gang issue disappeared tomorrow, there would be a lot of people looking for work.

This fact has not been lost on one perceptive Hispanic gangbanger. He says, "You [society] don't want to resolve the problem because it's a money thing. That's how I look at it. Citizens are making money because of all these gangbangers. Gang activity is one of the biggest moneymakers right now. Why get rid of the problem? In many police departments they have special units just for gang members. They're making money."

VIOLENCE

"The best part of being in a gang is beating those punks' asses."

—a Hispanic gangbanger

"Fukk all you crab-ass niggaz fu¢k u and to dat nigga clccs Pac WATcH yo azz watch yo muerr Phukkin ass B-doggzz moBBBin through kraB sETs. Pimps.In.Red. Uniformz fuKK all yall kraB wannaBees yall niggaz a'nt real yall don't know what a fukkin ghetto is. I'll hit you uP syde yo head until youre Brain leekz sHOUT OUT TAH ALL DA YG'S, OG'S, SG'S, & LIL PGS rePPrezentin dat 707 and all da Bloodz from tha Bay 2 L.A And all tha BLOODZ worldwide."

—from a letter written by a Blood gangbanger

(note the avoidance of using the letter C as a way of disrespecting Crips)

"Yeah, I think that we girls should be able to walk the street without being shot cuz of what color we wear."

—a black female gang member

"Make sure your vests are on tight."

—a black gangbanger to two police officers

"Fuck Asian gangs, esse. I be from East Los Angeles where

the real shit be. Mutha fuckers who think they be hard, try coming over my barrio and talk some of that crazy shit and get your ass stomped on by the crazy esses and the niggas."

—from a letter written by a Hispanic gangbanger

"I've seen too many funerals."

—a 10-year-old black boy to me as I stood guard at a Blood's funeral

"There are plenty of funerals in my neighborhood."

—a black gangbanger

"Gather round and join in
Break his jaw and crack his chin
Watch the teeth fall on the floor
Smash his head against your toe . . . Boot Party!"

—lyrics from *Boot Party,* by Intimidation One, a skinhead band

Citizens and even veteran police officers are frequently shocked at the callousness of gang violence. It's not uncommon for gangbangers (and even non-gang-involved youth) to shrug off a bloodbath as being no big thing. Detective Stu Winn says that often gangbangers put the lives of many innocent people in jeopardy when they expend dozens of rounds at a single target. "Many gangbangers are immature and selfish, not having developed any respect for human lives at their young age. They think only of themselves. They want what they want and don't care about anyone else."

Tim Clemmens agrees. "There does not seem to be any limits to the degrees of violence gang members will resort to. A look leads to a hand sign, a sign leads to 'mad dogging [a mean look],' mad dogging leads to insults, and that eventually leads to elevating levels of violence."

Veteran gangsters, called OGs (original gangsters), are often

Racist skinheads act out violently at a street demonstration by tearing and burning the American flag.

brazen and coldhearted, a result of having become calloused from years of gangbanging and having seen and done everything in the gang world. While many times the younger bangers do the drive-by shootings, Winn says he has seen a change. "Lately, I've been investigating a lot of shootings by OGs who want to get the job done right. Still, the younger ones are extremely dangerous because they have lots to prove."

All the experts I spoke with feel that gangs are more violent now. "There used to be rules," says one gang detective, "like you don't do a drive-by on a family house. But now they do it. I recently investigated a shooting where a gang shot at a house as people were coming out after a wake. Then they shot at other people down the street who had already left, and then they drove back and shot at the house again. In their minds, nothing is sacred today."

Jimmy Brown, a program administrator in the Department of Juvenile and Adult Community Justice in

Oregon, says that some of the old gangbangers, who are no longer involved in gangs and are now leading straight lives are shocked by how quick the new generation is to pull the trigger. "When I run into them from time to time, they tell me they are astonished by how quickly guns are used by today's young bangers. It used to take a lot to get the old-timers fired up enough to shoot someone. But now everyone is packing a gun, especially the 16- and 17-year-old kids, who use them at the smallest provocation."

Gang violence commonly occurs in places where young people typically hang out: parks, parties, street corners, school grounds, teen clubs, and fast-food eateries. Although these places are seemingly innocuous, the sad fact is that they often draw sudden and explosive gang violence. This is because when a rival gang is seeking a confrontation for revenge or for some other reason, they have no qualms about doing it wherever they find their targets, and often the targets are in places that are public. When a fistfight breaks out in a club today, there is an expectation in the minds of everyone present that someone is going to pull a gun—and someone usually does. And all too often, the end result is a lot of injured and dead people who were not even involved in gangs.

One gangbanger readily admits his heavy involvement in the lifestyle, though he is concerned about his loved ones. "But the worst part is when your family gets killed or shot," he says. "My little brother just got shot up, and neither him or me will ever be the same."

A Hispanic ex-gangbanger said that he got out because his family had been hurt. "I seen my uncle get shot, and it wasn't cool."

Violence is so explosive in some communities that straight people live in fear and are forced to exist like prisoners in their own homes. Some even sleep in their bathtubs, thinking that the tub will protect them if a stray round from outside penetrates the walls of their home. "In some areas,"

Jimmy Brown says, "you don't see people out in their yards, on street corners, in school yards, or in parks even on nice days. They don't think it's safe."

The concept of violence is kept alive by the way bangers communicate with each other every day. Joseph Marshall Jr. says that many of the words used by young people are associated with violence and death and may be responsible for some gangbanger's actions. He cites slang words like *hangin' out, chillin'*, and *illin'* as examples. "There are popular record labels called 'Deathrow,' 'Lynchmob,' and 'Kickin' It,' [the latter] which derives from 'kicking the bucket.' Eluding the cycle of violence becomes harder for young people, who react to these words, or other more destructive ones, without thinking."

ON GETTING SHOT

When gangbangers gather and the talk turns to the gang lifestyle, there is usually a ritual of showing off one's battle scars. Like old athletes pulling up their pantlegs to compare knee surgery scars, bangers lift their oversized sweatshirts to reveal a scar from a bullet wound (sometimes more than one) or knife wound (also sometimes more than one). There is a lot of bravado in the presentations, macho pride in being a member of a unique club of warriors who have been in battle. Retired Chicago police officer Jesse Beckom Jr., author of *Gangs, Drugs & Violence Chicago Style,* likes to slap young people with the reality of what it's like to get shot or knifed. He relates in his book what he tells them about the so-called "honor" of getting wounded.

> *Most young gang members are told by older members that it is a badge of honor to be shot or cut. These younger members are not well informed about the realities of being injured by guns and knives. . . . Gang members aren't told that 85 percent of those injured do not die but live with their*

> *injuries. In many cases, these young adults are left without eyes, legs, arms, or even sexual organs. . . . A bullet may enter the left shoulder, travel through the lungs, across to the right side of the body, hit a bone, ricochet down past the liver into the intestines and cause serious damage that might leave a person physically handicapped for the rest of his or her life.*

DRIVE-BYS

"I don't care what gang you in; if you talk shit you gonna get my AK-47 shoved up your ass."

—a black female gangbanger

"The lady said that she heard the shot and then saw the glass shatter all over her bed. She said she was too scared to even get up, so she just stayed in bed."

—from a news story

"County Sheriff's deputies are investigating three drive-by shootings. So far, there is no sign they are connected. One person has been killed, and two others were hurt."

—from a news story

"One of my best friends was shot and killed standing next to me. As respected and powerful as I was at the time, all I could do was hold him in my arms and lie to him . . . tell him he would live, when in fact, he was dead. My last words to my homie was a lie."

—a black gangbanger

When people think about street gangs, they get a mental image of a drive-by shooting, complete with black or Hispanic bangers slumped in the seats of a low-riding car, looking ominous in dark glasses and with colored scarves wrapped around their heads. One or more barrels appear out the side tinted windows followed by a rattle of automatic weapon fire. People on the street scream and drop to the sidewalk as windows and flower pots explode. If this image seems Hollywoodish it's because it's been depicted so many times in movies and on television. The reality is that drive-by shootings in the real world aren't much different.

Some gangbangers see drive-bys as their only option, especially since many of them don't think about alternative ways to deal with conflict. They think: "This guy dissed me, so I'll go get my shit and take care of business." They also think in terms of, for lack of a better word, custom. "This is the just the way we do it. We have always done it this way in the past, and we will keep doing it this way in the future."

All indications are that drive-by shootings are getting worse; in particular, more rounds are being fired today than ever before. "It's a new way of doing business," says one observer of gang warfare. "They use to just walk up and shoot, then over time they graduated to riding by on their bicycles and shooting, then they progressed to doing it from their car windows. Now they overdo it by shooting lots and lots of rounds. They just keep pushing the envelope."

John Miller says, "They spray everything with as many rounds as they can to intimidate their target. Of course, the weapon technology they have now makes it easy to shoot a lot. They just stick a MAC out the window and let it rip."

Detective Stu Winn thinks the shooters are simply immature. "There is nothing they hold sacred. Now it's load up and shoot like crazy."

WANNA-BE

"There is no such thing as a gang 'wanna-be,' and officials who use it should strike it from their vocabulary," says national gang expert Steve Nawojczyk, a retired Pulaski County Coroner in Little Rock, Arkansas, and an expert who has served as advisor to the Arkansas Attorney General's Youth Gang Task Force. "They're 'gonna-bes.' If that child thinks he's a Crip, he's a Crip. Calling gang members wanna-bes also lets people believe that 'we don't need to worry about it.' And communities do need to worry about it."

Like Nawojczyk, I've always had a problem with the concept of wanna-be, a name usually used by people when referring to kids on the fringe of being a gangbanger. "He's not really a gang member," claims the naive parent. "He's just a wanna-be." The school administrator, who is in denial that he has a gang problem on his campus, will say, "No, we don't have gangs on this campus. Oh sure, we have a few wanna-bes, kids who dress the part and talk the talk, but we don't have any hard-core gangs."

It's my opinion that this naiveté is one of the reasons gangs have gotten a foothold in so many communities around the country. The wanna-be label is vague, confusing, and too often used by people who are hiding their heads in the sand while gangs sprout up all around them like weeds. Here is a kid wearing gang clothing, talking the lingo, posturing, listening to the music, hanging out with others who are doing the same thing, and getting into trouble, all while hand-wringing adults, who can't see the obvious, are proclaiming, "Oh, he's a good boy, he's just a wanna-be."

Is there such a thing as wanna-be? Yes, technically. A kid who is hanging around a gang but has not yes been accepted—jumped in by the gang—is technically a wanna-be. He wants to be in the gang, but for whatever reason he has not been accepted.

It's important, however, that we don't ignore him or just shrug him off as not being a concern, not being a danger. He is a concern, and, in fact, he is often more dangerous than actual members.

"The dudes you have to be scared of are the guys we call wanna-bes," says one ex-gangbanger, named Angel. "They want to belong to a gang so bad, but for one reason or another nobody ever takes them seriously. The wanna-bes are the ones that will do anything to get some recognition from the gangsters. You give them a gun and point them in the right direction, and they will start blasting. They have no respect for anyone. All they want to do is belong to a gang."

We must never allow ourselves to of think of wanna-bes as kids who are simply playing gangbanger. The fact that they are have not yet been officially declared a member by a gang is what makes them try harder and, consequently, more of a danger. A wanna-be will often do whatever it takes to get accepted.

Wanna-bes behind bars are also considered dangerous by prison officials. Bill Valentine, a retired corrections sergeant in the Nevada State Prisons, says, "Wanna-bes are used as punks, mules, or are sent on impossible missions that may place them in grave danger. They are also used to hold weapons, drugs, or related contraband. Few are ever awarded total membership, but they are still used." Valentine says that it's not uncommon for a hard-core gang member to take a wanna-be into a shower stall and use him for sex.

DENIAL

"I'm not a skinhead," replied a shaved-headed kid wearing a flight jacket, red suspenders, khaki pants, and Doc Marten boots when I asked him about his affiliation. "I'm just making a fashion statement."

Sometimes it can be amusing as a police officer to have a tattoo-spattered banger, wearing all the regalia, with a half dozen of his buddies standing behind him—all of whom are dressed the same—tell you that he is not a member of a gang. While some are just playing with you because they know that you know who and what they are, others are trying to distract you because they don't want the police attention.

Hard-core gangsters, those completely into the lifestyle, are more apt to admit their involvement because they are proud of what they are and what they do. Those members who are not so deeply entrenched often deny their role for fear of getting unwanted attention from the police and, as a result, being documented as a gangster. Those who have yet to be accepted into a gang but are acting and dressing the part will either be frightened of the police and deny their involvement or they will inflate their chests with bravado and claim a gang set to "impress" the officers.

Erika Sylvester says that gang members deny their involvement more with a parole or probation officer because they want to impress the officer that they are living a straight life. "They won't show us their tattoos," Sylvester says. "If they do show them, they downplay what they mean, or they might come into the office wearing their colors but deny there is any significance to them. On the other hand, it's been my experience that the real hard-core will freely claim affiliation."

THE POLICE

"COP KILLER!
Yeah!
I got my black shirt on
I got my black gloves on
I got my ski mask on
This shit's been too long
I got my 12-gauge sawed-off
I got my headlights turned off
I'm 'bout to bust some shots off
I'm 'bout to dust some cops off
I'm a . . .
COP KILLER, better you than me
COP KILLER, fuck police brutality!
COP KILLER, I know your family's grievin' . . . FUCK 'EM!
COP KILLER, but tonight we get even."

—from the song "Cop Killer" by Body Count (w/Ice-T)

"The police are the enemy. The police are against the gang. There is a code that you do not talk to them. If you are taken to the police station, silence is your best bet. A gang-banger feels that the police will not help him, but will only put him away. A lot of bangers feel that the police are a legal gang itself, so they need to protect themselves by having as many guns as possible."

—a Hispanic gangbanger

"We get along with a few of the police who patrol our hood. There are a few who come by when we are hanging around drinking and getting high, minding our own business, and say hi to us and then keep on going. Others are real asses. Whenever we talk about the police, it's like we are talking about a gang that we are at war with."

—a black gangbanger

"If one disses me, I don't have any problem with taking out my nine [firearm]."

—a black gangbanger

"Cops are part of the problem. They all work for the Jews."

—a racist skinhead

"Cops are Nazis and go along with the racist skins."

—an antiracist skinhead

Like many criminals, most gang members don't accept responsibility for their crimes, but instead blame the police for their problems and for having their lives "messed up." Never mind that gangbangers did the drive-by. In their minds, it was the police who screwed them up by arresting them and taking them to jail. The police are responsible, not the gangbangers.

Timothy Clemmens concurs. "They seem to believe it is

someone else's fault that they injured someone or committed a crime. They don't take responsibility for any of it. If they fight, it's because someone else was disrespecting them by wearing a certain color, or they belonged to a rival gang. It's never the individual's fault for something. It's OK to shoot at someone or to fight them if that person did something the gangbanger doesn't like, whether the thing was done intentionally or not.

"Probation and parole officers are to blame when the juvenile violates his conditions for release from detention. Detention officers and rival gang members are to blame for everything when they get into trouble within detention. Law enforcement is to blame if they get caught for committing a crime. It never ends. Even the parents of the gang members take the same attitude. They say the system is harassing them or discriminating against their children. Rarely do the parents or the gang members ever take responsibility for their actions. The rest of us are simply people interfering with their lifestyle, and we are to blame for it."

Clemmens says that gangbangers, especially those who are hard-core, don't like interference in their activities. And they view the police as particularly interfering.

Detective Stu Winn says that some gangs look at the police with disdain. "The police are responsible for all the bad things that happen to them. Others like to talk shop, especially about weapons, because they think of us as living in their world. Some gangs look up at us as authority figures, though that doesn't mean they like us or won't try to hurt us."

When asked why more police officers and others in the justice system haven't been hurt by gangs, Winn says, "It just hasn't broken loose yet. But it seems like they are thinking about it more."

I asked John Miller the same question. He replies, "It depends a lot on the jurisdiction and the workers' attitude. In Portland, Oregon, anyway, there are few police brutality charges, so there isn't a pervasive disrespect for the police. That's not the case elsewhere."

Jimmy Brown, who has been working in Portland with Bloods and Crips since the late 1980s, feels that it's because "the police, parole and probation officers, and outreach workers use respect and good tactics when dealing with gangbangers."

It was my experience working gang enforcement that gangbangers think similarly to street hookers. Many hookers told me that it was their job to be prostitutes and my job to try and catch them at it. When I did catch them I always treated them with respect, and I seldom had a fight. They went along with their apprehension with an attitude of resignation that the stop, the arrest, and the trip to jail were inconveniences, but that was also just a part of doing business.

I found this same attitude to be true with *some* gangbangers. They know they have their role to play as gangbangers, and they know that the police have their role as enforcers. If a police officer treats a gang member with respect, the gangbanger will go along with the street contact or the arrest, though he doesn't like it and will still cop an attitude. But if an officer disses a banger or unnecessarily roughs him up, the officer is considered an asshole and open game to resist and assault.

Keep in mind that this acceptance of roles is not a phenomenon of all hookers or gangbangers. It's important, therefore, to never drop your guard when dealing with these people no matter how good a relationship you think you may have with them.

As you will read in the following chapters, veteran gang officers say that you will get more out of the bangers when you treat them with respect, something that every human wants, though gangbangers seem to want it twofold. For sure, you will get more cooperation with honey than with vinegar, but all the honey in the world doesn't always work. Believe me when

I tell you that it can be quite unnerving to find out, as I did once, that your name is at the top of a hit list. Me, Mister Nice Guy! This convinced me that it's not always about you and your charming personality, but rather the fact you wear a badge and all that that means. It's what you are that can get you hurt. Nonetheless, you are going to get more cooperation when you treat them as human beings. Many bangers get ego strokes from the attention they get from the police. They swell with pride that their local police agency has a specific unit, a gang unit, just because of them. The individual banger who gets extra attention from gang officers will get a boost in his rep from the other bangers. If the banger is wanted by the police, his rep soars because he is considered hard-core, and because he is seen as a fugitive, like those glamorous characters made popular by movies and TV programs.

There is much more about the police and the various ethnic gangs in the chapters that follow.

POSTTRAUMATIC STRESS DISORDER

Among counselors, outreach people, and others who work intimately with gang members, there is a growing discussion about the issue of posttraumatic stress disorder (PTSD) among youths who become involved in gangs. Jimmy Brown is one who has been looking at the issue. "What has changed from the services perspective is that we are no longer looking at the issue of juvenile delinquency just from the corrections orientation, but now we are looking at it from the mental health standpoint. When you look at delinquency through a mental health lens you see depression, PTSD, bipolar disorders, manic depression, child abuse, family involvement in the justice system, and many other indicators of risk. This is something we didn't do earlier; we just dealt with them on a probation level.

"But when you start looking at some of the underlying

causes of behavior, you begin to see some of the connections. For example, an anger management problem is an issue because the kid has seen so much violence in his life that it has now become his mode of operation in certain situations. He's seen Mom get beaten by Dad in the home, so he goes out and beats women. The way his family has dealt with anger was to get physically aggressive. So, when the kid's school teachers gets on him for not finishing an assignment, the kid gets in her face because that's how his family dynamics have always worked.

"So if you've got a group of kids who act out in school and they've been assigned to a room with other kids who are not focused in school and acting out, you have that bonding thing going on. Now you've got a group of kids with similar characteristics who don't like their math teacher, and the teacher doesn't like them. Since the kids don't play sports, don't dance or sing, they figure they can hook up and run together. Then when you have a bunch of depressed kids hanging around together, they are just waiting for something to help them blow it off. Then after a month, one of them says to the others, 'Hey, you know that one mother fucker over there? Well, he called me out. You got my back?' It's that kind of process that comes out of PTSD."

THE MEDIA

"I like to get media coverage because everyone will know who we are. The more people know who you are, the less they will mess with you."

—a black gangbanger

"I see the media in the 'hood and everybody goes, 'Hey, it's cool. We're going to get in the paper and everybody in L.A. is going to see us.' A friend of mine was on that *COPS* TV show once and he was really happy about it. He was going, 'That's me! That's me!' It's cool because being a gang member is about image, and when you got it, no one messes with you."

—a Hispanic gangbanger

Gangbangers and the gang life are glamorized in the media, which includes television, movies, and perhaps the most powerful influence of all, music videos. Hard-core rap artists "sing" about drive-bys, weapons, fights, illicit sex, gang camaraderie, drinking and drugs, shooting the police, and loyalty to the life. This popular music is in great demand by both white and black young people. Unfortunately, it provides them with negative role models as to clothing, language, and the gang culture.

Many bangers find the attention they get from the media to be a status symbol, solidifying in their minds that they are somebody. TV news in particular loves to do gang stories, especially color stories on individuals and incidents that proclaim dramatically that the gang problem is getting worse. Bangers love that stuff and strut around basking in their "celebrity" status, which has been given to them by virtue of TV news. They feel that their life has been validated because it's on TV, something that other kids never experience.

When I worked in the Gang Enforcement Team with the Portland Police Bureau, one of my jobs, besides working white supremacists, was to monitor gang graffiti. One summer, the city was virtually bathed in graffiti; it was as if all the gangs were competing to cover every blank wall. As one of the gang unit's media spokespersons, I asked several reporters to do a story on the huge problem as a way of educating citizens about how they could help the police and themselves.

They ignored the story for months until finally a newspaper reporter decided to do a big feature, complete with lots of photos of graffiti and interviews with taggers. When the story was finally published, it showed criminal taggers as romantic figures, moving about stealthily under the cloak of night, dodging the police and home and business owners, their pens, paint, and spray cans secreted in their backpacks.

I was enraged at the story's slant and wasn't surprised when the incidents of graffiti throughout the city escalated even more. The reason was clear, though not anticipated by the naive reporter: the taggers and gangbangers loved the attention they had received and the way in which they had been presented.

Officer Scott Gammon of the Gang Intervention Unit with Fort Collins Police Services in Colorado says that he too has found that gangbangers love the attention they get from the media. "After an article on gangs in the local paper failed to mention a specific gang by name, the gang went out the following night and left graffiti all over, scrawls that made reference to the paper's omission."

Detention Supervisor Timothy Clemmens feels that the media glamorize gangs and thus advertise the lifestyle to impressionable young viewers. He says that when the media show a banger flashing a hand sign, they are actually broadcasting a diss to the signer's rival gang.

Pamela Sowers says gangs love the attention. "They go by the credo that all media attention is good for market share, so they like having their gangs named in the media."

Detective Jack Simington of Kennewick Police Department in Washington state is quite adamant in believing that the media are a big part of the problem. "If the media didn't print the names of the gangs, it would help diffuse the retaliations and deny the gang's existence. Without acknowledgment or endorsement for the gang, it just becomes another crime in the newspaper or on TV."

Bill Valentine bluntly says how the media contribute to the gang problem in prison. "The media contribute enormously to the problem. Recognition! The media, the entertainment industry, inmate activist groups all supply the craved-for attention. The bangers slop it up. Rap stars and other entertainers make millions of dollars catering to the gangbanger mentality."

Several gang officers tell of finding news clippings of shootings and other gang activities tacked to bedroom walls. Some bangers even own scrapbooks of news clippings of crimes they and their gangs have committed, and some have acquired the police reports that were made by officers after their crimes. Gangbangers on parole or probation, however, don't like attention from the media because they are trying to appear innocent to their parole officers.

I can recall several occasions when antiracist skinheads would call a press conference about an issue, or call a specific reporter who had given them a business card, and give the time and place of a demonstration. All four channels would show up, and the antiracists would get their faces and quotes on the evening news. This dramatically escalated their sense of importance and boosted their numbers with other young people seeking attention.

THE MENTALITY BEHIND THE SPREAD OF GANGS

As mentioned earlier, street gangs are no longer just a big-city problem, as gangs large and small move into small cities and rural towns all across the United States. This disease-like spread is a result of susceptible youths accepting gang propaganda that comes at them from a number of places.

Perhaps the primary way in which small-town and rural youths are exposed to gangs is through contact with established big-city gangbangers in youth detention facilities. When local youths who are having problems with delinquency are mixed in with hard-core gangsters from the big cities, they are almost a shoo-in for everything that the world of gang involvement has to offer. Once exposed, the small-town youths quickly gain an education in gangbanging and, seemingly overnight, develop a much harder, big-city banger attitude. After their release, they return to their small towns, but now they have big-city gang ideas. Additionally, many of them maintain contact, social and business, with the big-city bangers they met while incarcerated.

Gangbanging often spreads to small towns when a big-city banger moves or visits a friend or relative there. It's quite common for families in cities like Chicago, Los Angeles, and Portland to send their gangster kids to stay with an aunt or a grandmother in the country, hoping that the new and sedate environment will chill out the kid. Unfortunately, the kid takes with him his gang knowledge, his gang mentality, and all his personality traits that are part of gang involvement. He then hooks up with rural kids who are already getting into trouble or are looking for something to replace their negative home life. In short order the local kids are gang affected, and the big-city visitor has himself a gang. When the kid returns to the city, he has a connection for his dope trade and other gang activity.

Small-town and rural kids are not immune to the gang information they get from the movies and music videos. While kids in these remote areas are not exposed to gang dress, language, attitude, and crimes for real, the movies and music videos give them their education. Add to this a kid who has, for whatever reason, criminal leanings, and you have a self-taught gangbanger.

DO GANGBANGERS WANT OUT OF THE GANG?

"Without gangs life would be a lot less violent."

—a black female gangbanger

"It's hard for me to say what life would be without gangs."

—a black gangbanger

"Life wouldn't be too much different without gangs 'cause you still do the same shit wit' the same boys."

—a Hispanic gangbanger

"Even if you get a job, several guys will come over to you and start talking about gangs. White people will ignore you, but the first guys that will come up will be black and Mexican. They'll go 'What's up? Hear you from East L.A.'"

—a Hispanic gangbanger

"I think life without gangs would get boring sometimes. Some of us bangers only know how to run the streets."

—a Hispanic gangbanger

"I think without gangs my life would be boring. But there's a catch to being a gangsta. The catch is that you could die, get hurt, or lose time in your life from going to jail."

—a black gangbanger

"It's hard to get a job, especially if you are Hispanic or black. That's why lots of them sell drugs. They might try, but then someone comes over and they start drinking and the person says, 'Let's go do something,' like a crime, and then suddenly you're right back in it again."

—a Hispanic ex-gangbanger

"Some gangbangers might get out, but they still carry that seed with them."

—a Hispanic gangbanger

It's not easy to get a gang-committed banger out of the lifestyle, especially kids in middle school and high school. Some require psychiatric counseling for their drug abuse, behavioral disorders, and the trauma they have suffered from all that they have seen and done surrounding their gang activity. In particular, female gangbangers or hangers-on (some only associate with gangs because that's where the boys are) who have been passed around sexually will experience psychological trauma. It's not easy getting them away from gangs because there is tremendous peer pressure involved, as well as the usual rebellious teenage mentality and the attitude of the banger's family, which may be apathetic, antiauthority, or also gang involved.

Scott Gammon believes, as do many people, that given a choice, most gangbangers would choose a different direction for their lives. However, since this lifestyle is the only way for them to feel wanted and recognized, they continue to belong to the gang. "Many of them become institutionalized," he says, "meaning they don't know how to live outside of the gang lifestyle. Those who come out of prison may want to make a change, but they don't know any other way but the gang way."

Timothy Clemmens believes that bangers definitely want out, especially if they are parents. "Even though most gang members state they will never leave their gangs and that they will be loyal forever, they always want something better for their children. Most of them have their own kids by the time they are 16, and this may be a maturing experience. Usually the most violent crimes are committed by gang members under the age of 16 who are still trying to prove themselves and build a reputation. Once they get past this age, they begin to learn that there is a better way. Unfortunately, by this time it's too late for most.

"In a way, these juveniles are just like other people. When we have a new job with new friends, we try hard at first to be accepted, be liked, and do a good job. We rarely attempt to find a new job until we are comfortable with the one we have. Once we are comfortable, we look for ways to improve our income and our position in life. For these kids, they need a gang to save them from their home lives, but once they are comfortable they begin to see that there may be a better way of life out there. Sixteen is basically the turning age, and if there is hope for them, they will begin to change at this point. Those who don't end up career criminals.

"Oddly enough, this is also the age where kids can begin to drive, so maybe they don't feel as limited as before. Maybe they see that they will have more freedom and control of their lives and won't have to depend on the gang as much as before."

CHAPTER 2

BLACK GANGS

"I'm banging for pleasure, power, money, and respect."

—a black gangbanger

My partner and I were assigned to baby-sit a dead Crip lying peacefully in his coffin in a funeral home. He was on display for family, other loved ones, and fellow gang members to come by and have a look and say good-bye before the funeral the next day. Our job was to ensure that the Bloods didn't come in and vandalize him or his coffin or disrespect him in some other way.

We parked our car around back and took up a post in a couple of plush chairs in the lobby. It was a gray, misty November day, as gloomy outside as it was inside the funeral home. The funeral director was in an upstairs office, so we were basically alone in the place, except for the Crip, who we could see lying in the semidark room that adjoined the lobby. Soft organ music wafted from somewhere.

We had been sitting there for more than an hour when a low-rider pulled into the gravel lot and cruised slowly to a space near the door. My partner and I both became alert, not knowing if the black face we saw inside was a friend or foe of the deceased. A second later, the biggest human being I had ever seen uncurled from the driver's side and stood up and up and up.

"Big one, isn't he?" my partner understated. "Name's Jerome. Stands 6-feet-6, tips the scale at 310. Don't worry, he's a Crip; name's Biggy, friend of our proned-out friend."

Biggy stood beside his ride for a moment, turning his head left and right and then looking behind him, like a hunting dog trying to pick up a scent. He was wearing a tent-sized blue T-shirt cut off at the waist and blue shorts that hung so low they exposed at least 12 inches of his white boxers; the bottoms of his pantlegs touched his ankles. The top of his shorts were stretched over his ample hips, and the ends of his belt, which he couldn't fasten, stuck out like rabbit ears. To keep his shorts from falling all the way to his shoes, he clutched a wad of waistband in his hand.

He looked like an idiot, and my partner and I giggled like school children as he be-bopped, complete with an Elvis Presley sneer, across the empty lot toward the lobby door. When he pulled open the glass door, his eyes widened in surprise at seeing us standing in the lobby, but he quickly regained his Elvis sneer and added an antipolice attitude. Clutching his pants, he ignored us, held his huge chin high, and be-bopped across the lobby and into the viewing room. A few minutes later, he passed us again as he crossed the lobby and then went out the glass door.

What impressed me about this otherwise uneventful five minutes was that Biggy was not performing for anyone when he climbed out of his car and walked into the funeral parlor. There were no other cars in the lot, and there was not a soul out in the misty weather, and he didn't know we were there until he walked into the lobby. Nonetheless, he still sagged his shorts so low on his hips that he had to hold onto them to keep them from falling off, he still affected a gangbanger strut, and he still wore his badass sneer.

He didn't do any of this to impress others, but he did it because that's who he was. He was a gangbanger through and through, a real hard-core, and, as such, sagging, strutting, and sneering are part of what it's all about. When he saw us, he didn't stop his antics, nor did he add to them. He just continued carrying himself as before. I remember thinking that I wouldn't be a bit surprised to learn that he did the same when he was alone in his own home.

Three months later, Biggy died in a hail of bullets fired by his own Crip gang. The shooters have never been caught.

A BRIEF HISTORY

The first black gangs that formed in California during the 1920s were loose associations, mostly unorganized and rarely violent. They didn't mark graffiti on walls, use monikers, flash hand signs, or do any of the other gang identifiers we see today. Gangs then consisted mainly of family members and neighborhood friends. Compared with what is happening now, their criminal activity was minor, though it was still designed to present a tough image, earn respect, gain a reputation, and make easy money.

From 1955 to 1965 black gangs increased in size, operating mostly in South Central Los Angeles and in a nearby area called Compton. They grew as more and more black youths bonded together for protection from them and from other rival gangs that were also growing in number. It was a circle feeding on itself, and from it the Crips and Bloods were born in the late 1960s.

The Crips first formed in southeast Los Angeles and developed a reputation for being the fiercest and most feared gang in L.A. as they terrorized local neighborhoods and schools with assaults and strong-arm robberies. Other black gangs formed at the same time to protect themselves from the Crips.

The Bloods were first seen around the area of Piru Street in Compton, California, which is why they are sometimes called Piru. At first the Bloods were outnumbered about three to one by the Crips, but they nonetheless earned a reputation as being an extremely vicious street gang, and they have endured to this day.

Both the Crips and Bloods divided into numerous and smaller gangs, called *sets*, during the 1970s, but held onto the names Crips and Bloods. They quickly spread throughout Los Angeles County and began to claim certain neighborhoods as their territory, a process that was violent and bloody. By 1980 there were thousands of Crips and Bloods in and around Los Angeles.

Today, gang sets range in size from just a few members to several hundred with little, if any, organized leadership. The typical age of members varies from 14 to 24. Initiation into a gang, getting jumped in, may include fighting other members in the gang, committing a crime, or assaulting a rival gang member.

Gangs remain territorial and highly motivated to protect their neighborhoods from rival gang members. They establish unique symbols, such as colors specific to their gang; monikers, such as "Mad Dog," "Shotgun," and "Cop Killa"; graffiti that identify the gang and individual members; and hand signs that form letters unique to the name of their gang.

Drive-by shootings began in the early 1980s and remain a popular way to carry out revenge or simply have a thrill. The buying and selling of illegal narcotics was minor prior to the 1980s, but by 1983, black L.A. gangs jumped on the crack trade, along with marijuana, LSD, and PCP. And the money began to flow.

During the 1980s black gangs began migrating to other U.S. cities, large and small. Some of the migration was the result of normal movement by families, but most of it was

Black male and female flash gang signs.

purposeful by gangs who wanted to introduce crack cocaine into virgin territories. They succeeded, and now black gangs are found in small cities and even in rural areas.

In the upper Midwest and some places in the South, black street gangs fall under two rival umbrella groups: People and Folks. These two groups represent a collection of individual gang factions with specific dress, symbols, speech, and so on. One observer described the situation as analogous to Major League Baseball teams that belong either in the National League or American League. It's a similar situation on the West Coast with Bloods and Crips, which are also umbrella groups for hundreds of sets.

It should be noted that while Folks and People are mostly found in the Midwest and Bloods and Crips are mostly found on the West Coast, they are seen all over the country now. There are Bloods and Crips on the East Coast and Folks and People on the West Coast. The gang business requires that they move around.

OK, that's the basic history in a little more than 25 words. If you are interested in more detail, there are lots of books, as well as articles in magazines and information on the Internet. But our purpose in this chapter is to examine how black gangbangers think. So let's begin with their thoughts on respect.

RESPECT

"Respect is huge with them. For some gangbangers, respect is all they got because they live in filthy houses, their mom's a hooker or strung out, and the banger has no job or much of an education. So when he leaves the house and goes out into the 'hood, it's like, 'Hey, here I am.'"

—Detective Doug Justice

"I've investigated shootings where black bangers have hunted down a guy who had mugged him [gave him a hard look] and shot him. They will pull out a gat [firearm] right there in the street and start blazing. All this just because they got mugged."

—Detective Stu Winn

"Respect is closely related to reputation. The way others show respect for a gang member, or how the banger reacts to a lack of respect directed toward him, will influence his reputation. The more violent his reputation, the more others fear him. Rep and respect are power to gangbangers."

—Timothy Clemmens, detention supervisor

"They get prestige and esteem from driving a nice car and wearing those nice clothes."

—Detective Stu Winn

"Respect is necessary for a gang member to succeed in what he believes success is."

—Detective Jack Simington

Detective Doug Justice relates an experience he had that illustrates the significance of respect among black gang-bangers. "On one occasion, a gang officer named Brundo, who stands well over 6 feet tall and threatens the bathroom scale at 240, was sitting in his patrol car talking to a half-dozen Crips who were gathered on the corner. At one point in the conversation, a big Crip named Gat told Brundo to shut up. When Brundo opened his door and climbed out, the other bangers stepped back a few feet, leaving Gat and Brundo standing toe to toe and face to face.

"Gat looks nervous but to save face he says, 'If you didn't have that gun belt on, I would kick your ass.' Well, big Brundo raises his eyebrows, unsnaps his gun belt, drops it onto the seat of the police car, and looks at Gat with an expression of expectation.

"Gat's homies are lovin' it, and they call out to him, 'What are you going to do now, Gat?'

"Ol' Gat's mouth is twitching a little now, and his left eye is watering. He mutters, 'I ain't doin' nothin', man. He's the police.'

"Brundo's eyes are like burning into him, and he's smiling as he says softly, 'If you ever want to go one on one, you just let me know.'

"Well, Gat's homies just erupt with catcalls at him. They are totally dissing him, saying things like, 'You big pussy' and 'Hey, man, he even took off his gun belt' and 'I can't believe you didn't do nothin.'

"This went on for weeks. Every time Brundo drove by the corner, Gat's homies would start in on Gat again. Respect for Gat hit rock bottom."

While removing the gun belt isn't a recommended police

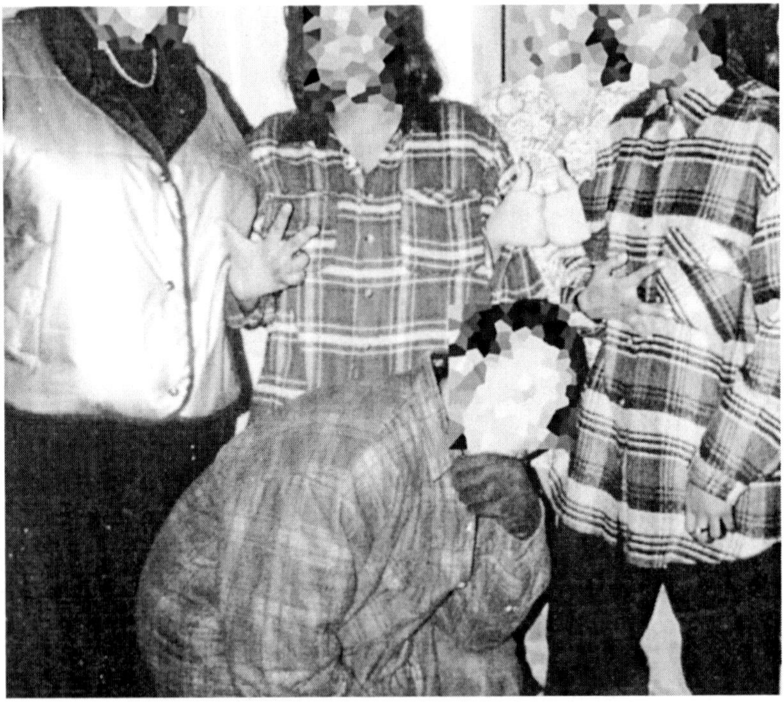

The gang and respect are all some bangers have.

tactic in the presence of gangbangers, this time it worked. Officer Brundo's rep went all the way to the ceiling because the bangers respected the cop who didn't cower in front of them.

Another officer told me a story of how he got respect from a black gangbanger, a method that would freak the administration and all the do-gooder groups, not to mention that it was a tad illegal. The method worked because, as many officers told me, gangbangers respect force. For obvious reasons I won't use the officer's real name. Suffice it to say that he works in a large city in the Midwest and has nearly a dozen years working with street gangs.

"I pulled up to this Crip corner," he says, "where four young cops were just standing there doing nothing as this big

Crip named Jerome was berating them in the worst way. He was running around in circles, holding up his middle fingers and screaming, 'Fuck the cops! Fuck the cops!' There were a bunch of other Crips standing around laughing their heads off at Jerome and dissin' the cops, too.

"I couldn't believe these young officers were just taking it. Then Jerome ran over to me and stuck his middle finger in my face and screamed, 'Fuck the cops!'

"I reached out and snagged him by his throat and dumped him onto his back. I slapped him a couple times and banged his head against the curb. Then I asked him, 'Now, what were you saying about the police, Jerome?'

"Well, Jerome looked at me with big eyes and coughed out in pain, 'It . . . was . . . a . . . mistake.'

"I told him to never again say and do those thing when I pull up. I told him that I don't drive by and say, 'Fuck the Crips,' so you don't say, 'Fuck the police.' He kept rubbing his head and saying, 'All right, man, all right. It's cool, man. It's cool.'

"Well, all his guys were laughing at him because I threw him down on the sidewalk. It had an effect on Jerome because he knew that I wasn't going to tolerate him cussing and dissin' me. We set the tone early, and I never had any more problems with him."

REPUTATION

"You can't fuck wit tha Folk Niggas."

—a Folk gangbanger

"Reputation is everything. It ultimately evolves into recognition for the gang member."

—Detective Jack Simington

"Rep is what carries a banger through the 'hood. If he's a good fighter, good with women, and got a good car, his rep will get to the party before he does."

—Detective Doug Justice

"Black gangbangers try to dress more macho than white kids so as to try to look like a badass, which helps establish their reputation."

—a gang observer

"Reputation is everything to black gangsters. You earn your rep by being a badass, by whom you beat up, whom you kill, and how much time you spend in jail."

— Erika Sylvester, parole and probation officer

"Rep is very important in their peer group and among other gang members. It gets them in doors that other kids can't get into. It lets them live bigger than life. It precedes them into the community and allows people to see them as powerful, especially inside their own peer group. It acts as a shield and allows the gangbanger to get around outside his group. But his rep also causes him to be a victim."

— Jimmy Brown, juvenile and adult
community justice administrator

"Its importance is extreme to them, especially among the young ones. They have to act dangerous, crazy, scary, usually toward another person. It's also important for their survival so that no one will testify against them."

—Officer Mike Stradley

"A gangster's rep is of the upmost importance to him. His reputation has the same significance to him that decorations on a uniform have to a soldier. Many gangsters have been abused or neglected at home, and most have never been truly cared about. They don't want to be hurt or forgotten again, so they perform the same acts as the others in the gang to build their reputation. It's a sign of their strength and achievements, and for the first time these juveniles have something to be proud of. They will do anything to keep this feeling and maintain their reputation."

—Tim Clemmens, detention supervisor

Many gangbangers have grown up (if you call reaching the age of 14 or 15 being grown up) in poverty, within dysfunctional families and suffering from a lack of education. For some of them, their rep is all they have; it's their source of identity. "I am the crazy dude who will shoot anyone," one banger says of his rep. Their status or rank within the gang, sometimes called "juice," is based to a large extent on the rep they establish for themselves. The gang they belong to establishes its rep in the outside world, and they have to maintain that rep by continually acting out as well as by exaggerating stories of their activities.

The rep of gangs is often used by those not involved in them. For example, it's common to hear a black and sometimes a white child under the age of 10 years say when being picked on in the school yard, "Hey, leave me alone. I'm a Crip! I'm a Crip!" Although he has no gang affiliation, in his young, impressionable mind the child hopes that the reputation of the Crip gang alone will scare off his antagonist.

A 10-year-old may get away with falsely claiming membership, but gangs don't take lightly older youths doing it. There have been many cases of people being seriously assaulted for claiming a gang when they weren't members.

REVENGE

"Revenge against a rival gang member is common and expected to maintain the respect that has been given them by fellow gang members."

—Detective Jack Simington

"A banger's gang will give him shit if he doesn't get revenge when he's been dissed. They may even beat him up."

—Detective Doug Justice

"It's common for them to justify their actions by saying something like, 'Hey, I was the victim. I wouldn't have done that drive-by if they wouldn't have done that to me first.'"

—Erika Sylvester, parole and probation officer

"In prison retribution must be swift and exact, otherwise the prison gang member loses face and in turn becomes a victim of other prisoners."

—Sergeant Bill Valentine

"Reputation, revenge, and respect are interwoven in their minds."

—Detective Doug Justice

There is an expectation in the black gang culture that revenge is an automatic response to being dissed in some fashion. The individual gangbanger who doesn't do it will find that his life in the gang suddenly becomes miserable. The dissed banger will be hassled, teased, and called a punk. He will not be allowed to hang out with his homies or party with them, and he may even be beaten for his inaction.

Jimmy Brown says that revenge is linked to reputation. "When a gang member is victimized, it's his reputation that leads to that victimization. A Blood will say, 'I know he is a Kerby Block Crip, and I know that he carries a gun. It's nighttime now, and he's out there. I'm going to get him.'

"And so the Crip gets shot at. That's the initial stage of victimization. The second stage is that because the Crip got shot at, there is a likelihood that there will be another crime, another shooting. The Crip will say, 'He shot at me and nicked me; now I'm going to go and shoot at him.'

"Revenge is always extreme with these people. It's never, 'I'm going to go and break out the guy's window.' Rather it's, 'I'm going to go and break his head.' It falls back on the reputation. They are thinking, 'How am I viewed in the world? I can't be seen as soft.'

"When you talk to a kid in a counseling session and ask how the conflict can be settled peacefully, the kid says, 'There is no way to do it with peace. The conflict is there, and revenge is going to happen, maybe six months from now, maybe a year from now. But it's definitely going to happen.'"

Jimmy Brown says that their lack of planning makes it difficult for law enforcement to act proactively. "The gangbangers whom I've worked with don't sit up in a room and plot out how they are going to get revenge on a guy. They don't say, 'OK, he always walks on this street,' or 'He always shoots hoops over there. Let's get him at 10 o'clock on a Saturday night.' They don't think that way. The reality is that it's very situational with them, so it's hard from a law enforcement perspective or from a corrections perspective to do something about it. Of course, we know that there is always going to be some kind of retaliation after a big incident, and it usually happens 10 days to a couple of weeks later."

BELONGING AND IDENTITY

Commandments of the 'Hood

- Thou shalt not snitch.
- Thou shalt handle thy business.
- Thou shalt do what thou gotta do.
- Thou shalt get girls.
- Thou shalt get thy respect.
- Thou shalt get thy money on.
- Thou shalt carry a gat.
- Thou shalt be down for thy homeboy, right or wrong.

"How old are you?"
"Seventeen, homes."
"How you livin', man? Are you in school?"
"Fuck no, I got kicked out, homes."
"You got kicked out of school?"
"Yeah."
"Why is that?"
"Cuz I was knockin' people out, dude."
"You gotta chill with that, man. What are you going to do without an education?"
"I don't know. Just sell drugs or somethin', bro."

—A counselor's conversation with a black gangbanger

"I don't think the ones who are 14 and 15 want out yet. The older ones who have been through a lot and are getting tired of it are more likely to want out."

—a gang outreach person

"There seems to be a shift now as to how they see themselves. They think more now about what's in it for me. What can the gang do for me? It's more about greed and the dope trade."

—Officer Mike Stradley

"In many black gangs, to become a member, you must be jumped in by members of the gang. This entails being 'beaten down' until the leader calls for it to end. Afterwards, all gang members hug one another to further the 'G thing.' This action is meant to bond the members together as a family. Frequently, young gang members, whether hard-core or associate, will talk of fellowship and the feeling of sharing and belonging as their reason for joining a gang."

—a prison official

"The wearing of colors is not as big in their minds now. Now they war over girlfriends and dope as opposed to fighting over clothes."

—Officer Mike Stradley

"A real misconception that many people have about big-city gangsters is that they all run around with Uzis, wearing Oakley sunglasses, blasting everyone in sight while snorting huge heaps of coke. On a nationwide basis, about 38 percent of gang members are actually involved in drug dealing or distribution or major crimes for purposes of income. The rest are gang members who use the gang as a support mechanism in place of a real family. The gang offers belonging, recognition, and a sense of accomplishment. The gang meets basic human needs that more normal youths find at home."

—a gang observer

Jimmy Brown feels that the young person who is forced to join a gang is more dangerous than the one who joins out of choice. "The kid [is] forced into a set and begins thinking about how he is going to make a reputation for himself, how he can show that he has heart. In the early days of gangs, we were always challenged to determine who was hard-core as opposed to those who were new at banging. What we figured out was that the hard-core were just those kids who already had a long history of juvenile crime. Gangs were just another stage of their criminal development. The newer ones were not as criminally involved. They got into it out of fear and for self-protection. That made them more dangerous because their perception that there was someone out there lurking for them made them more quick on the trigger.

"They are also quick to carry a gun. We have kids out there who are packing weapons who have no prior history of doing so. But other kids, those from well-known criminal families and who have been doing crimes for a long time, aren't always packing. They have access to them, but it's the 14- and 15-year-old kids who more commonly have the guns."

Brown doesn't think that today there is the glamor associated with having a special police unit formed to target them that there used to be. "In the early days of gangs," he says, "a lot of kids thought it was cool that there were gang cops out there. Now in some of the larger cities, they're used to seeing that. The smaller cities that are just now forming gang cops may find that to be the case, but not the bigger jurisdictions."

Brown says that it's difficult for many bangers to get out because there are so many steps to the process. "First, the kid has to answer the question, 'How can I get out and not lose face with my homies?' Second, we know that the kid most

This banger's sense of identity can be seen in his colors, foot position, the angle of his right arm, and the gang sign he is flashing with his right hand.

Gang member displays his gang acronym on the back of his jacket and stands in a gang stance.

likely is not going to move to some remote area that is gang free because he doesn't know anyone there. From a service approach, when we consider taking kids out of the gang lifestyle we have to consider the environmental issue, the peer group issue, the taking of the kid's essence, the things that the kid has been focused on in the gang and the community, and then try to replace it all with nongang, positive things."

Tattoos

Most black-gang tattooing makes some reference to their gang and their homies, not only indicating their affiliation but their loyalty to the life and their role in it. Included in the tattoos is the following information:

- Gang name
- Set name
- Street name
- RIP (rest in peace) followed by a gang member's name. Sometimes there is a drawing of a tombstone.
- Five-pointed star, five dots: possible People gang affiliation
- Six-pointed star: possible Folk gang affiliation
- Street name, which indicates the significance of turf
- Drawings of weapons: handguns, automatic rifles

THEY LIVE IN THE NOW

"Sometimes we plan things, but mostly when things come up, we do it without thinking. Like I would be walking to a party and see a car at the curb with keys in it. I wouldn't think about going to jail or getting killed by the car owner. I would just take it; I felt totally free."

—a black gangbanger

"You get in my way, and I'll take my auto and shoot your ass."

—a threatening female gangbanger

"If I die, that's just the way it is."

—a black gangbanger five minutes before he was killed

Like other youths involved in gangs, most if not all black gangbangers live in the now with little thought about the repercussions of their actions. Many of their disagreements are over dope or women, and in their minds the best way to settle the problem is with a gun. I asked one gang expert why gangbangers go to the extreme of shooting people over the slightest provocation. He replied that taking out a gun and firing rounds at a person is the only way they know how to solve their problems. "It's because," he said, "that is just the way they do it. They don't problem-solve. They shoot."

Detective Doug Justice agrees. "A beef can start out as a verbal disagreement and can escalate [snaps his fingers] just like that. For example, recently at a backyard barbecue two bangers started arguing over something, and a minute later both of them lay dead on the grass after shooting each other."

Detention Shift Supervisor Timothy Clemmens says it's the "smile now, cry later" philosophy. "They don't think; they just react," he says. "Most of the violent crimes committed by gangbangers are spur of the moment. They use whatever weapon they have at that second in time."

Detective Jack Simington says, "They don't think. They have total disregard for human life, theirs and innocent bystanders. They will do anything for glory and recognition."

Bill Valentine sees the same thing in prison. "Bangers in prison are more violent today than ever before. They are more inclined to assault officers, and they have little fear of reprisals."

VIOLENCE

"You're a scared little beaner. When I find you, I'll cut your fucking balls off and duct tape them to your mouth. Then I'll kidnap your spic mother, and I'll shave her head and make her suck my fucking dick for a couple of hours. And if you have kids, I'll stick my knife in their ass and suck the eyeballs out of their head."

—an angry black gangbanger
threatening a Hispanic banger

"If I die, I die."

—a 15-year-old black gangbanger

"A few members might be sitting in a restaurant when a boy walks in with the brim of his cap tilted to the right—a possible sign of Crip or Folk loyalty. I'd say to him, 'Why do you wear it like that?' and ask him to straighten it or tilt it to the left like mine. If the boy gives the wrong answer, there would be a battle. If the other boy is first to pull a gun, it doesn't matter. If you're there for your cause, you don't think about that. One day you're going to die anyway."

—a black gangbanger

"I remember thinking as I was going out to commit a crime or to just bang that I had to look good just in case I got killed. I didn't really care if I got killed because it went with the territory. But I wanted to look good if it did happen, and I didn't want to die crying or looking scared. If you were going to kill me, kill me and go on."

—an ex-gangbanger

"They live in a culture of guns and violence more than other criminals. Some bangers say that they won't live to see 20."

—Detective Stu Winn

"Most say to me, 'I'm not going to make it to 20, so I may as well be the baddest I can be."

—Officer Mike Stradley

"They tell me all the time that they don't plan to live past 25."

—Erika Sylvester, parole and probation officer

"Most regard their fate as something beyond their control. Their death and the death of their homies is an accepted thing."

—Sergeant Bill Valentine

"They get drunk or high and start talking about getting someone. They are on an adrenaline high. But then when they go to do it, their loose plans go to pieces."

—Officer Mike Stradley

"I'm 17, I've lived my life."

—a gangbanger when asked if he was worried about getting killed by another gang

"I always carry a gun. Somebody could end up doing something behind your back."

—a black gangbanger

"Yo, I am in Folk [set name deleted], and if anyone wants to talk about us you can kiss my ass and come my way if you want to die."

—a Folk banger

"All of y'all that are Bloods are punk-ass Niggas wouldn't be talking shit wit a gat in your mouth. Come down my way and we'll see who gets fucked up."

—an e-mail from a Crip

"I am a Blood killing all these fools in blue. We all red causing these blue bitches to be dead. We are five-star elite Niggas busting on these Niggas' domes."

—a female black gangbanger

"I left the gang unit because I saw so many dead kids, sometimes just minutes after I had been talking with them."

—Detective Doug Justice

Recently, the Office of Juvenile Justice and Delinquency Prevention funded research in Ohio to track leaders of gangs to see what happens to them over time. They discovered in

Columbus, Ohio, that juvenile criminal activity began with minor property crimes and progressed to violence against people.

During the 15-year study, they monitored 83 gang leaders who accumulated 834 arrests. The researchers identified a clear pattern of arrests in each of the five gangs they were watching. They found that a gang's peak arrest for property crimes occurred about a year and a half before its peak arrest for violent crimes, which was followed by a peak for drug crimes three months later. The researchers theorized that violent crimes increased as the gangs began engaging in drug activity.

The researchers also found that the increasingly violent activities took their toll on the gangs: by the end of the period studied, a disproportionate number of the gang members, relative to the general population, were dead.

Erika Sylvester says that it doesn't take much to trigger rage in a black gangbanger. "They have no sense of conflict resolution skills, and they are especially volatile if you get in their face or diss their set or their peers."

Gang detective Stu Winn says that black gangs have changed over the years—for the worst. "It takes less to tweak them now. There is nothing sacred anymore. Now it's load up and shoot like crazy from a car or just walk up behind someone or stalk them for a little while and then blow them away. If they are drinking somewhere and a fight breaks out, someone almost always pulls a gun."

Jimmy Brown says that the "old-timers" are telling him that they think the young ones are too trigger-happy. They say that it used to take a lot for a gang to get riled enough to do a drive-by or some other form of violence. "Now they do it easily. They will walk up to someone and shoot, or they do a drive-by in a car. Sometimes they even do a drive-by shooting from a bicycle. And their weapons are getting heavier and heavier. Everyone, especially the 16-year-olds, are carrying guns. The envelope keeps getting pushed. It's not surprising

"So Many Tears"—a gangbanger wears a T-shirt in honor of a slain comrade.

to me anymore to see gangbangers go into a restaurant and shoot everybody up.

"They see everything in black and white; there is very little gray in how they view their world. When someone shows disrespect, it will quickly lead to a confrontation. There is very little chance in discussing how to resolve a conflict nonviolently. It's always resolved in the extreme. You don't get much chance for thinking, 'Let me think about this thing a little bit more. Are there other ways to solve this as opposed to using violence?' The reality is, 'You called me out, so I'm going to get my shit and shoot you.' They have a real fatalistic viewpoint. That's also why you don't see a gradual increase in violence, but rather extreme, explosive violence. A kid will say, 'The dude yelled at me, so when I saw him later walking down the street and I happened to have my gun with me, I just shot him.' It's this kind of thought process that makes kids in gangs so dangerous."

Jimmy Brown says that a lot of violence comes from issues around girls. "A gangbanger will say, 'Somebody's girlfriend did somebody at a party,' or 'She used to be my girlfriend, but now she's running around with somebody else.' I hate to say that male-female relationships are at the bottom of a lot of violence, but in many situations it has been."

Brown feels that many of the bangers have a sense of fatalism they can't avoid. He says, "Gangbangers think, 'This is the way it is, this is the way it always has been, and this is the way it will always be.' There is no way out. There is an acceptance that if you are born on [name deleted] Street, then you are automatically a [name deleted] Street. This has been the case in places in like Los Angeles for a long time. Now we see it in the smaller communities, too."

Other experts say that most gang violence is centered around narcotics, but in Brown's experience drugs don't seem to be a big issue with the younger bangers. "I see that more with the young adults, 21 to 28, who are selling dope and using the younger ones as their protectors or their muscle. But I don't think there is as big of a connection among the younger ones as a lot of people want to say."

As a juvenile detention supervisor, Timothy Clemmens has found that most of the violent crimes performed by gangbangers are on the spur of the moment. "Whatever weapon they have when they meet someone will be what they use against that person, whether it's a rock or a gun. But then there are times they will not push the issue, and it will lie dormant so long as they don't see that person. However, once they do see him, the anger will be just as severe."

Clemmens says that black gangbangers don't think, they just react. "While seeking vengeance or attempting to gain respect from the gang, a banger will simply shoot first and ask questions later. I don't know the sociological reasons for that. If it's family or a fellow gang member, they will do everything to protect him or her. When the person isn't a family member, they don't care. Sure, they will be sorry later if something happens that they didn't plan on, but that won't deter them from doing it again in the future. It ties into that sociopathic 'smile now, cry later' mentality."

Tim Clemmens works closely with bangers every day and has found them to be extremely fatalistic. "Most gangbangers don't see a future. They don't worry about it or expect things to ever get any better. If they have to risk death or serious injury today to get something, they will not worry about getting shot tomorrow. Logically, if you are in a gang, you have to realize there will be pain and suffering and maybe death near you. It would be better and safer to avoid this type of lifestyle. However, members don't see this. Their belief is: What can I achieve today regardless of the consequences? They don't want to die or be injured, but most will not make the changes necessary to protect themselves."

For sure, most young gangbangers see a dismal future and think there is little they can do to make a change. Most have had a lousy family life, a poor education, and see little opportunity in their immediate future other than crime. This makes them angry at the world in general, at those more affluent and educated, and depressed over a future they feel they have no control over, one that is already set for them. Since they don't see anything happening in their present and certainly nothing down the road, they perceive the gang as a way out or a way to be somebody. Mix this mind-set with all the violence that fills their world, and you have an armed, volatile kid with a fatalistic attitude.

THE POLICE

"They can smell a new cop a mile away."

—Officer Mike Stradley

"They need to know that if they diss a cop that something will happen."

—a police officer

Everyone I interviewed feels that the relationship between black gangs and the police is getting worse. As gangs move toward greater violence and more firepower, it's only logical that there will be an increase in violence against police. Detective Doug Justice remembers when there used to be a sort of mutual respect between bangers and police officers. He says he would chase a gangbanger over hill and dale and when he finally collared the guy, the banger might not like it, but there would be an acknowledgment that the police had won. He says this didn't happen in every police-banger contact, but overall, there was a sense that gangbangers recognized that there were roles being played by each party.

"Now they try to set up the police," Justice says. "I know that they often talk among themselves about ways to get the police, like on a traffic stop or during a foot chase. When you flip on the overhead lights, they try to stop in a specific location, a place where they can deal with you."

Many officers said that gangs are thinking and planning how to react when the police interrupt their movement. For example, when an officer approaches a group on a corner or pulls over a carload, the faster banger is given the dope, and he runs off through the blocks. Other times, the dumbest one is given the evidence to run with, unaware that he is being sacrificed by his homies. Gang Officer Mike Stradley says that they know the police will always chase the one who runs. "Often, the guy who runs is the guy who doesn't have a warrant. The wanted guy stays in the car and then either takes off in the car or takes off on foot as soon as all the police are off chasing the guy without the warrant. Inevitably, the car contains the dope and guns, but it's gone when the winded cops return."

Detective Justice says that bangers are even running differently now than they used to. "They used to just run a block or two, hide, and we would set up a perimeter to flush them out. Now they run seven or eight blocks because they know we can't set up a perimeter that fast or that large."

Officer Stradley tells of another new technique black gangs are doing. "Another tactic they have planned and are putting into action is to return to the car during a foot chase and drive away. The driver will run away in a straight line, and the passenger will run off in a large circle. Then the passenger will work his way back to the car and leave with it before the backup officers get there."

Several officers told of situations where the bangers run through the blocks and then try to position themselves so they can ambush the police. This sort of strategy isn't new in places like Los Angeles, where black gangs have been entrenched for a long time, but it's happening now in smaller cities and in suburbia where gangs are increasing at an alarming rate. Although it's been mentioned in this book several times that gangs have a tendency to react explosively and spontaneously, it's becoming apparent that some black gangs are planning to some degree how they will react when confronted by the police.

Although big cities are experiencing attacks on police officers by gangbangers, smaller jurisdictions have not reached that point—yet. They may have incidents where a gangbanger will fire at the police to prevent apprehension, but there is not yet an all-out war against the police. With the passing of time and the emergence of a second generation of gangbangers, who knows what will happen? New bangers might be more willing to prove themselves, and veteran bangers might believe they have little to lose.

In many cases, black gangbangers know the police as well as the police know them. They know who are the "good" officers and who are the "bad" ones. "Some cops they hate and some they tolerate," says Officer Mike Stradley. "I have found that you have to get their respect, and most often they only respect police officers who have the ability to get physical. Force is something to be respected in their minds. If you give them too many breaks and never make them toe the line, they will laugh at you behind your back and take advantage. You have to force them to respect you, and even when you get it, you have to keep in mind that they are still dangerous.

"When they don't like an officer, it's often because the officer doesn't treat them as an individual. I also make them understand that officers are all individuals, too. I tell them that I recognize that they are all individuals and that I am not going to treat them badly because another gangbanger treated me like shit yesterday. I tell them that how they treat me is how I will treat them. I say, 'Let's have a mutual respect. But, hey, if you want to treat me like shit, that's OK, because I'll treat you like shit, too.' I tell them it's their call."

Young police officers often have a hard time when they first work the 'hood. White officers in particular may not understand the black culture or the gang culture. Detective Doug Justice says, "Younger officers often have a fair amount of fear in their new environment, so they put up a real strong front, an attitude of 'you do what I say' with very little conversation that is give and take. Bloods and Crips see cooperating with the police as a very bad thing. They won't even cooperate with us to put a guy who shot them in jail. For example, I'll say to a Crip, 'I know who shot you, and you know who shot you. If you cooperate with me, I'll put him in jail, and you will get your revenge on him.' But inevitably they will say no, not because of some great plan to get revenge, because that doesn't always happen. They say no because any cooperation with the police is like admitting that they need them to help, and in their mind, that lowers them to punk status in the gang.

"I talked to a banger in the hospital the other day who had been shot in the back during a drug rip-off, the bullet paralyzing him from the chest down. He knew who shot him, but he says to me, 'Yeah, I know who did this, but I'm not going to tell you. We'll take care of it.' In his case, he probably will have it taken care of by his homies. But even in those incidents where payback doesn't happen, the banger's reputation will soar when he refuses to cooperate with the police and doesn't lower himself."

John Miller says that black gangbangers tell him that most police officers don't want to talk to them but just want to hassle them. "If they would only stop and talk, they would be seen as OK, and they would be respected because they would be just doing their job."

The bangers Jimmy Brown works with say the same thing. Brown says, "Some of them have created a sort of strata. At the top are good cops, and at the bottom are bad ones. The good cops just stop and talk; they're OK. If the cops understand them and don't diss them in front of their homies, the bangers tolerate that and can handle the contact. But if the cops leap out of the patrol cars and get in their faces, they are ranked low on the strata and won't get any cooperation or information.

"You don't have to buy into their value system. When you're just talking to a kid on the street who hasn't broken any law, you don't have to put yourself at a high, extreme level in your approach. You can just stay low and have a discussion with the banger. Treat him as an individual and treat him with respect."

When Brown talks about respect, he's not saying that officers should respect the banger's lifestyle or his crimes. He is saying to simply treat him as you would any human. Remember, gangbangers put a lot of stock in respect. Play to that and you will get much more out of the contact than if you leap from your car and scream in his face.

Doug Justice says that it's important to talk with bangers person to person and to make sure they understand the rules. "Don't pussyfoot around with them. Tell them, 'If you do this, then I'm going to do this.' Don't try to be their buddy; they don't like it. Everyone should know their roles. They know you're the police, and you know they're the bad guys. You can be on a first-name basis or use their little nicknames. But when you cross over that and do a high-five with them or talk their gang talk, they laugh behind your back. They want to honor the police officer/gang member roles. They have their job to do, and you have yours, sort of like the coyote and the sheep dog. You punch in on the clock, hit the street, and you expect to see certain bangers out, and they expect to see certain cops out. They're going to try to sell their dope, and you are going to try to catch them at it.

"Be careful about dissing them in front of their group, like screaming and yelling at them and shoving them around. You'll knock the banger down in his standing, and you will never get any cooperation out of the guy the next time you're at the scene of something. But if you have a fight with the guy—say he hits you and you hit him back—and you win, that's cool with him and the gang, because you're both playing your roles and you were fair.

"If you do have to jump on a particular banger about something, call him over away from his gang. For example, tell him, 'I don't yell at you in front of your homies, so don't you yell at me like you did yesterday, making cracks and laughing when I drove by.' You get the message across without embarrassing him."

Detective Stu Winn says that if you make yourself worthy of their respect they will talk to you more. "They will cooperate with a specific officer if they think he is 'straight and true.' Some might cooperate if they think it will get them less time in the joint, but there are others, and you can see this clearly in their faces, who just want to kill you. They see you as the enemy who is responsible for what has happened to their buddies."

Winn, who has been working gangs since the late 1980s, has noticed a significant change over the years in the cop-gangbanger relationship. He says simply, "We are seeing them take us on more now with guns."

CHAPTER 3

HISPANIC GANGS

> "I hope one day all this madness will end."
>
> —a Hispanic gangbanger

A BRIEF HISTORY

Hispanic gangs began forming in California during the early 1920s to gain strength in unity and to socialize in the Hispanic barrios. There was no formal structure or leadership among the members, who were all male and between 14 and 20 years of age. They did commit crimes, but mostly against property, such as burglary, and various types of vandalism.

As is the case today in many parts of the country, the gangs were defenders of their barrios and would fight to protect them. There were violent clashes between rival gangs over turf issues and any number of other violations, real or imagined. They fought with fists, feet, knives, zip guns, chains, clubs, and bottles.

Just as they do today, early gang members committed crimes as a way of gaining status in the gang and respect in the barrio. They found that a nice side benefit of having an established rep was that when the banger was sent to the California Youth Authority or the California Department of Corrections, his status in the gang was already established or, as one banger put it, "his rep preceded him."

Things got worse over the years, and by the 1980s Hispanic gangs were actively targeting their own communities and neighborhoods for drive-by shootings, assaults, and murder. Gang fights evolved into gang wars. As violence became a way of life, the original concept of protecting the barrios became secondary or lost completely. The gangs became organized and structured, with leaders emerging from the ranks of older members, called *veteranos.* As new members were recruited—some 12 years old, some as old as 40—the veteranos taught them the ropes of gangbanging.

As gangs have evolved over the years, the bangers have established unique tattoos, hand signs, names, and graffiti. Tattoos and graffiti depict the initials or the name of a gang and the banger's loyalty to it. The graffiti mark their territory and send messages to rival gangs. Hand signs form the letters of the gang's initials and are used as a greeting among members of the same gang and as a way to diss a rival gang. A member chooses a moniker or is given one by others in the gang, and it's usually kept for life. All of these actions are designed to show gang allegiance, bring a sense of cohesiveness to the gang, and, as mentioned, antagonize rivals.

Today, there are thousands upon thousands of Hispanic gangbangers throughout the country, many of whom are second- or third-generation gang involved. Their sets vary in size from a few members to several hundred. They are still involved in typical gang activity (in fact, two weeks ago two Hispanic gangbangers were gunned down in a drive-by a few miles from where I'm writing this), but they have evolved into entrepreneurs in the narcotics trade. In doing so, and out of necessity, their arsenals have expanded to large-caliber hand-

Although most people think of Bloods or Crips when they think of gangs, there are more Hispanic gang members in the United States than there are black gangbangers.

guns, shotguns, and automatic weapons, which has led to even more violent crimes.

A few of the Hispanic gangs have accepted members from other races, and some Hispanic gang members have joined other ethnic gangs. In some places, various Hispanic gangs have aligned with other ethnic gangs from the same neighborhood to have more protection from rivals.

Hispanic female gangs have evolved out of all this and

have done their share of drive-by shootings, assaults, vandalism, and auto theft.

Although black gangs receive the most media attention, Hispanic gangs and gangbangers far outnumber the Bloods, Crips, Folks, People, and other black gangs. In some areas of the country, Hispanic gangs are increasing faster than all the other gangs mentioned in this book *combined*. Contributing to the rapid growth of Hispanic gangs is the rapid growth of Hispanic populations in some areas of the country; a high dropout rate in high school; and, as is seen with all gangs, denial by parents, schools, and communities.

Some people think that gangs in general have a certain mystique about them, given their clothing, the gang vocabulary, and the crimes they commit. Hispanic gangbangers are often seen as having an even greater mystique about them because of the language barrier and certain aspects of their culture.

Let's examine how Hispanic gangbangers think and see if they are indeed all that different.

RESPECT

"I joined because people would think I was hard."

—a Hispanic gangbanger

"If you don't have any respect, you don't have anything. This is the way it is when you are gangbanging. If you step in front of me in line or cut me off in the street, you'll get a beating, and if you get an attitude about it, you might end up dead."

—a Hispanic gangbanger

"If a dude is talking bad about me at a party, I will find him and stomp his ass. If he was out somewhere talking trash about me, he will be taken out. You don't think about the police or anything."

—a Hispanic gangbanger

Even behind bars, a Hispanic gangbanger's respect is all important.

Like other gang members, Hispanic gangsters want respect, and they will go to any extreme to get it. They will act out so as to be perceived as the craziest and most feared member in the gang. Some want to be seen by others as having a *vato loco* (crazy life). Some will tattoo three dots on the back of their hand to indicate *mi vida loca* (my crazy life).

Louie Lira, a former Los Angeles gangbanger who now works as a gang specialist with the Youth Gang Program in Portland, Oregon, says that a gangbanger has to earn his respect; he doesn't automatically get it because he is a member. "You are not going to get it just because you killed 20 or

30 guys. You have to earn it by doing lots of things and by how you conduct yourself. I know 60-year-old gang members who have been in it forever but still don't get any respect. A guy may have done a lot of shootings and done time in the penitentiary, but if he has a big mouth, he isn't going to get respect. But another guy may do two years in prison, but he'll get respect because he has earned it doing good things for the others and good things for the neighborhood."

Louie says that a good rep can be destroyed easily. "You can do something cool like a shooting or prison time, but then you can do other things that will wipe it all out. Like if you give dope to a guy and tell him to go sell it for you, but when he does and you don't give him a cut, you ain't going to get no respect. Or if you got a nice house and car, but you ain't taking care of the baby homeboys or homegirls (young bangers), you won't get any respect. You don't get respect just because you act tough and crazy; you get it by taking care of your homeboys."

Hispanic ex-gangbanger Albert (he didn't want his last name used) says that respect is usually shown to a banger's family, though not always. "If you are walking with your mother at the mall and some gangbangers see you, what happens depends on how you act. There is a certain line they won't cross, but it depends on you. If I turn around and say, 'Hey, what the fuck you lookin' at?' they will see that I don't have any respect for my family. They will beat the crap out of me right there or do whatever they got to do. But if I have respect for my family and I see some bangers, I will keep walking. They might look at me and say something, but as far as trying to beat up on me, that probably won't happen."

REPUTATION

"Civilians in the 'hood were always scared of us."

—a Hispanic ex-gangbanger

"You are no good without some kind of rep, so that's when the rapes, shootings, robberies, and stealing come in. Even if it's drinking until you can't move, the rep plays a big part in how you will be treated in a gang. You have to do something no one else has done or go further than the last man."

— Sandra Davis, ex-gangbanger who now works for Mothers Against Gang Wars in Los Angeles

"Reputation is the only thing that you got. Your life don't mean shit without it. If my mom is going to go to court to testify on a case that affects my gang, I've got to get rid of my mom, because that is going to create a bad reputation for me."

—a Hispanic gangbanger

"The younger ones coming up are trying to prove their name and their status of where they're at in the gang. So they jump in the car with their crew, and they go looking for somebody to shoot or to beat somebody up."

—a Hispanic gangbanger

"Rep is all you got. You want to be known as crazy and down so that everyone will want to hang out with you. Sometimes you act crazy for protection, too. If I'm known to be crazy and hard and I go to prison, everybody is going to know me there. I don't have to go through that breaking-in period in there."

— Albert, a Hispanic ex-gangbanger

Louie Lira says that a banger's reputation is as important as his life. "Rep is the main rule. You gotta act tough even if you don't want to. You gotta keep your mouth quiet at all times because if you say something wrong, you will destroy your rep and the rep of the whole gang. Other gangs will look at your gang as snitches, and they will lose total respect for

A Hispanic gangbanger's reputation lies in his look, his gang affiliation, and his actions.

you. It will create a big problem on the street and in the penitentiary. Inmates will find out that you snitched out on the street, and your gang inside will pay the price. They will find this out even before you get inside."

Louie Lira says that snitches are not always treated poorly. "In some parts of the country, snitching and turning state's evidence are tolerated among Hispanic gangbangers. They might point you out as a snitch on the street and in prison, but they won't do anything to you. A young Hispanic will say that he won't kill someone because he knows he will get 25 years to life. I guess in some areas they put more value on human life than in other parts of the country. But if you snitch in California, for example, and you get sent to jail or prison, they are going to be dealing with you right away, not three years from now, but right away. When you say to a dude in California, 'Hey, why don't you go and kill that guy?' he'll say, 'Good idea. I'm going to go and do it right now.'"

REVENGE

"Revenge against a rival gang member is common and expected to maintain the respect that has been given by fellow gang members."

—Detective Jack Simington

"Retaliation at its deadliest can mean the murder of the rival gang member, and it usually happens in a drive-by shooting."

—a gang observer

"You snitch, and they will kill your mama or baby brother."

—a Hispanic gangbanger

"I've seen bangers seek revenge even when it wasn't clear to them what the rival did. They just know that it's expected of them to get payback. When I've asked them what caused the extreme hate, they couldn't answer. The original insult may have happened years ago, but they still have the need for revenge."

—a police officer

"There is no value to human life unless the gang member is directly related to the victim or he is a homeboy."

—Detective Jack Simington

"Sometimes a gang will get revenge against a guy who doesn't want to be in the gang anymore. One time a guy said that to the Mexican mafia. They didn't say nothin' to him then, but when he left the gang, the next day his wife is dead, two of his sisters are dead, and the three-month-old baby is dead."

—a Hispanic gangbanger

Ex-gang member Ruben Alvarez talked of the adrenaline rush he had after being shot at and the urgent need he had to strike back. "I remember sitting in a fast-food place with one of my homeboys. As we were talking, these guys from a rival gang saw us in the restaurant, and they got out of their car and came up to the window and started shooting into the place at us. They didn't hit anyone, but I can still remember how I felt. I was alive, and all I could think about was revenge. I came so close to dying that night, but all that was going through my mind was finding these fools and hurting them."

As we have seen with some Hispanic gangbangers, the absolute need to strike back, the duty to retaliate for being wronged in some fashion, is an unsatiated hunger. The banger may plan his revenge, or it may just happen when the opportunity presents itself, as is the case with most incidents of gang violence. The banger may get wronged in June, but the opportunity to strike back doesn't present itself until December. Over the months, the anger festers just beneath the surface, so that when the banger is presented with the moment—say the rival shows up at the same Saturday night party, or is seen on a street corner, or is spotted sitting in a parked car—his rage explodes and people get hurt.

BELONGING AND IDENTITY

"Many Hispanic gang members live a separate life on the street [than the one in] their homes. They are a gangbanger on the street, but at home they will have a wife and three kids. They place value on the family. In my experience, they seem to lean toward having nice families."

—Detective Stu Winn

"To us, it was all about how we presented ourselves to other gang members. We kept our clothes clean and our pants highly starched. I even ironed my T-shirts with pleats. Our shoes were polished, and our cars were clean. I wanted to look good just in case I got killed."

— Ruben Alvarez, ex-gangbanger

"Wow, if everybody sees this [graffiti tag], I must be important."

—a Hispanic gangbanger

"Hispanic gangbangers see themselves as outcasts."

—Alberto, ex-gangbanger

"When a youth joins a gang, he is looking for his or her place."

—a Hispanic gangbanger

"While most black gangbangers will deny their involvement to their parole and probation officer, Hispanic bangers more readily claim a gang."

— Erika Sylvester, parole and probation officer

"I am very heavy, and when I went to elementary school I wanted to be loved and accepted by my peers. Well, it didn't work out that way. I was talked about and humiliated by the students. But there was a group there that was very negative—they dissed the school, the policies, the teachers, other students, the community, and their parents. I found that by hanging out with them, I didn't have to hear the name-calling as long as I followed their negative behavior and was part of the group."

—Sandra Davis, ex-gangbanger

"The gang makes me feel secure and accepted."

—a Hispanic gangbanger

"I would rather go back to prison because there ain't shit out here for me."

—a Hispanic gang member

"Everybody wants out, but it's hard."

—a Hispanic gangbanger

"Most who are forced into a gang have a leaning that way to begin with. They usually have an OG [original gangster, meaning a veteran banger] pushing them to be violent."

—a gang unit police officer

"There were just a few gang members who were really down. I figure that maybe 5 to 10 percent of the guys were truly hard-core. This is a small number when you think of all the guys who gangbang. The hard-core are gone; there is no turning them around. But the other 90 percent are just in it for the ride."

— Ruben Alvarez, ex-gang member

"Look at me. My mom was a gangbanger, so for me it was like a way of living. After my uncle got shot and got put into a wheelchair, my mom got out and begged me to get out. I told her not to trip."

—a Hispanic gangbanger

"Gangbangers wear a certain type of clothes so other bangers know who they are. They take pride in how they look."

—a Hispanic gangbanger

"Some may want out of the gang and may even move out, but they carry the seed with them in their minds."

—Albert, Hispanic ex-gangbanger

"There is an aspect of suicide among many of these gang kids (between 10 and 21 years old) whose options have been cut off—no education, no work, and no opportunities for advancement. They stand on street corners and parks, flashing gang signs, inviting bullets. It's either *la torcida* (prison) or death: a warrior's path when even self-preservation is not at stake. And if they murder, the victims are usually the ones who look like them, the ones closest to who they are—their mirror reflections. They murder and they're killing themselves, over and over."

—Joseph Rodríguez, writer and photographer

Louie Lira says that when he was banging, he was in denial as to what being a gang member really meant in the scheme of things. "I was in denial; I thought I was better than other people my age. I didn't realize that I wasn't shit. I was jealous of other kids who said they were going to college. I never told them this straight out, but I really was jealous. So I acted stupid. A lot of us had an opportunity to do those things, but we blew it away. We were just like those other kids: we had parents, and we had what they had. But we chose the easy way because we thought banging was cool.

"There is a change in California now. A lot of the gang members are going back to college to get their career or a degree because they feel jealous. We are not dumber than the straight kids. Some of the bangers have talent, and they are fucking smart. I'm smart. If you give me land, I'll build you a house from the ground up, and I can fix any car, engine, and body work. There are straight kids who go to college, and they can't do that shit. I'm jealous of those guys because maybe they can't do this shit that I can, but they still got the paper. I got to get my GED and a college degree, just so I can go out and say I got the paper. Then I'll feel better. Without it, I'm just another fucking loser.

"Gangsters feel that they are a bunch of losers, but they won't admit it. That's why they act like that because they feel that they fucked up. You hear bangers say so many times that the system failed them. Bullshit, they fucked up. They know it, but they try to blame it on something else. But there are some bangers who tell kids to go to college and be somebody. 'Don't be like me,' they say. 'Don't be a fucking loser.' But

"Wow, if everyone sees this, I must be important."

bangers want the money now. They want the easy way out. Money motivates people."

Most Hispanic gangbangers are 100 percent loyal to their gangs and are so consumed by them that they will maintain their loyalty to the death. Their membership is who they are, what they are about, and what they exist for. Most experts say that Hispanic gangbangers are more mentally entrenched in the gang life than are black gang members. Although the gang format provides the young Hispanic his identity and a feeling of belonging to a family—the same as it does for other ethnic gangs—it is for the Hispanic a complete approach to life; for many of them, banging is not something to do just to hang out. Some believe deeply that the gang is even more important than they themselves are.

Louie Lira says that he has asked police officers and other people if they are willing to die for what they believe in. "Hispanic gangbangers are," he says. "They are willing to take it to that level. I've seen bangers hold their arms out to another banger with a gun and say, 'Go ahead and shoot,' and mean it. Hispanic gangs are more loyal than any other gangs. You can be a Crip in one place and then move and be a Blood in that place. With Hispanics, you are in that gang for life. Just because you left your hometown and moved to a different town that don't mean shit. I left California 10 years ago, but if I went back tomorrow, people there would say, 'Yeah, he's still in the same gang.'

"I don't do any gangbanging anymore and haven't for a long time. But I don't call myself an ex-gangbanger because I'll always be a gang member. The only difference is that I don't do what I used to do anymore. Sometimes I'm out on the street and I get approached by a banger who says, 'Hey, where you from?' and I'll jump at him like I used to and say, 'Hey, mutha fucker, what's wrong with you?' Then I'll stop and say to myself that I'm not doing this anymore."

Tattoos

Hispanic gang members take their tattooing seriously, and many of them cover their bodies with elaborate and sometimes beautiful art. Here are a few typical Hispanic tattoos that indicate how they think.

- *Mi vida loca*. (My crazy life).
- 13, X3, XIII, *trece,* any other form of 13. The gangbanger with some form of 13 tattooed on his body is probably from Southern California or at least he identifies with other bangers there.
- 14, N, XIV, X4, *catorce*, any form of 14. The gangbanger with some form of 14 is from Northern California or at least identifies with bangers there.
- Three dots in a variety of patterns stands for *mi vida loca.*
- The banger's gang name, such as "18 Street." This shows loyalty to the gang.
- Religious art. This doesn't automatically mean the person is a banger, but many bangers wear it.
- The head or the head and body of the Aztec warrior. This tattoo indicates the banger's warrior spirit.

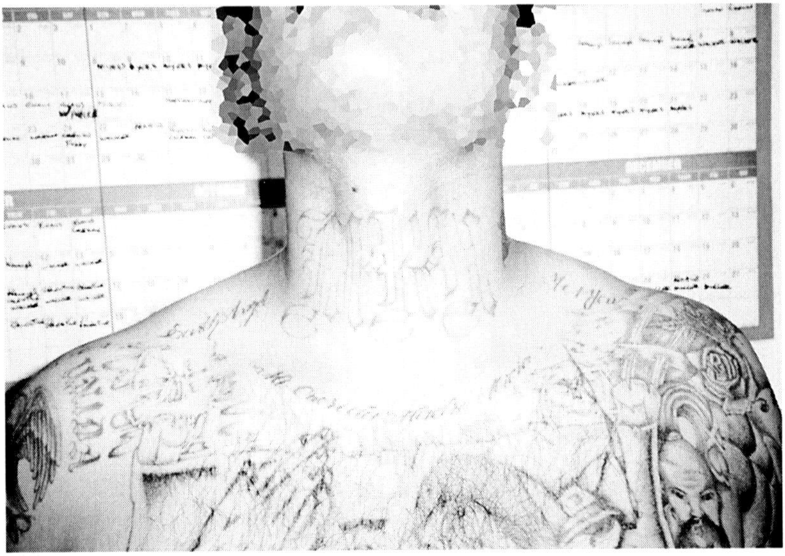

Hispanic bangers often cover themselves with elaborate tattoos.

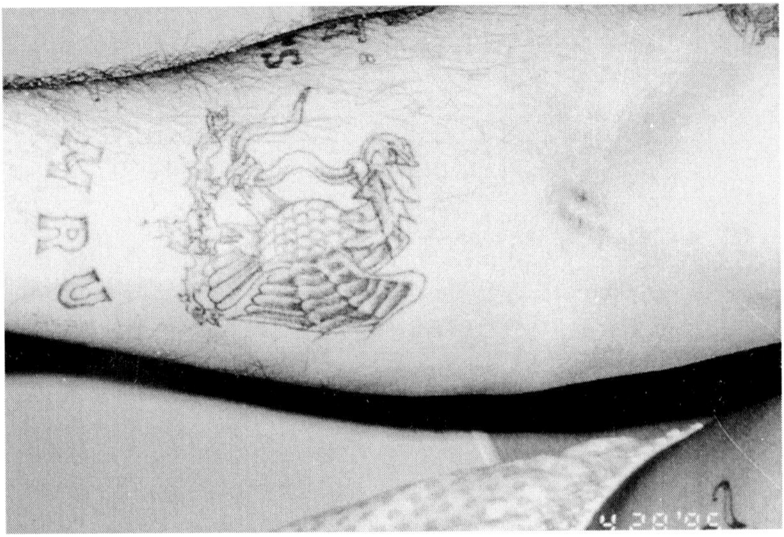

MRU: *Mi raza unida* (my united brothers). Note the heroin tracks on this Hispanic gangbanger's arm.

ACTING IN THE NOW

"We used to plan burglaries and holdups, but mostly things would just come up and we'd do it without thinking. I know how wrong that is now, but then I loved it. If I saw something that I wanted, I just took it."

— Ruben Alvarez, ex-gang member

"They get drunk and high first, then go do their violence. Everybody will be in a park and drinking and doin' dope, and then everyone will jump in the car and go do a drive-by. A lot of times they get stopped later for DUI, and the cops find the gun. So they get caught because they are drunk. Like one time this friend of mine sits in this restaurant with his wife and another guy, and he gets really drunk. Then he tells them that he is going to rob the place. So he does it, but the police catch him just down the street a few minutes later. I just heard that he's getting four years to life."

—Albert, Hispanic ex-gangbanger

"You don't think about it while you are doing it, even when you are doing it for five or six years. But now I wake up in the middle of the night and wonder, 'What the fuck did I do? How many mothers' hearts did I break? How many kids did I leave without a family?'"

—Louie Lira, Hispanic ex-gangbanger

"I'm going to die anyway, so why not shoot heroin?"

—a Hispanic gangbanger

Teenagers in general act like there is no tomorrow. They may have a great family, do well in school, and associate with other positive, non-gang-affected people, but by their very nature they are spontaneous, often acting as if there is nothing beyond the moment. Teenage gangbangers carry this further because of the nature of gangbanging and any psychological problems stemming from their home life and their experiences in the gang.

TURF AND SYMBOLS

"I'm not in a gang anymore, but I still claim my turf for life because I've always been taught by friends not to turn against my street and never turf hop."

—a Hispanic gangbanger

Many Hispanic gangbangers have a mental attitude that they are protectors of their turf. As one gang cop said, "If you give a hard-core Hispanic banger a stool and tell him that it's his turf, he will stand on it and fight to protect it from anyone who comes near." Many of them live by the motto "To die for the dirt," meaning that they will fight for their turf against rival gangs, the authorities, and anyone else who ventures across their boundary lines. Their turf is where they exist—it's part of their identity, and, for some, it's their entire world. Some gangs even claim names that relate to their turf, such as "Pine Street Cholos," "Eastside," "Southend 13," and "18th Street."

Louie Lira says that symbols are everything to the Hispanic gang member. "It's like the president of the United States has the American flag symbol wherever he goes; the difference is that he's not willing to die for it. But a Hispanic gangbanger will tattoo his symbol on the side of his neck and then go walking down the street in a rival gang neighborhood. Some might say he is stupid or just doesn't care, but to me I know that he knows the consequences and is willing to die for it. Symbols mean a lot to us; without them we would be lost because we wouldn't have our identities.

"Younger bangers may not even know the importance of the symbols. They just think it looks cool. Sometimes you'll see a kid with 13th Street on the side of his neck, and you'll ask him what it means. He says, 'It means I'm crazy for the life.' Well, bullshit, that's not what that means. They just use symbols without really knowing what's going on. Later they want to remove it, because they didn't think about the consequences or they weren't serious about it or they didn't even know what they were doing."

The banger look is also used to intimidate. I was riding a commuter train off duty late one evening when a half-dozen Hispanic bangers scrambled aboard. All of them wore khaki pants, white T-shirts under long-sleeved flannel shirts that were buttoned only at the top, and hair nets. All had tattoos on the side of their necks and on the backs of their hands. The ride was uneventful except for their rowdiness and the fear that was clearly etched on the faces of the other passengers. Even as a seasoned police officer, I have to admit the look was intimidating. That's why I sat with my hand inside my jacket, resting on the butt of my friend, Mr. Glock.

POLICE, CORRECTIONS, PAROLE AND PROBATION, AND DO-GOODERS

"These people who come out here and try to help us, they're bullshit."

—a Hispanic gangbanger

"When do-gooders would talk to us and try to get us out of the gang, we would just listen politely and then go do what we were doing before."

—a Hispanic ex-gangbanger

"It all depends on where the parole or probation officer's head is and how his first contact with the banger is. Unless the banger is given something to do and is interested in it, he will just continue to hang out and be part of a gang."

—Sandra Davis, ex-gangbanger

"Most gangbangers don't like the police because everything the gangs are doing is illegal. They also don't like them because they stop them all the time for doing nothing. Like in the Los Angeles Police Department they got the CRASH unit, and they always stop us, even when I've had my little son in the car."

—Albert, Hispanic ex-gangbanger

"Some cops are just doing their job; there are good ones and bad ones."

—a Hispanic gangbanger

"The only reason we didn't go to war with the police is because we were told by the old gang members that if we did start something the cops wouldn't let up until we were all dead or locked up. And it would hurt all of our criminal operations."

— Ruben Alvarez, Hispanic ex-gang member

"When I get stopped, I just sit there and be quiet and not say nothin'. I don't want no ass-kickin' from a cop."

—a Hispanic gangbanger

"A lot of gangbangers feel that the police is a gang itself."

—Sandra Davis, ex-gangbanger

"Some Hispanic bangers almost look up to the police as an authority figure. There is some of that respect left over. I'm not saying they are not dangerous, but when they have to deal with the police, they sort of yield to them as an authority figure. But it's important to keep in mind that not all of them do this."

—Detective Stu Winn

"I think it's funny that we would always try to be invisible to the police, but then we would tag every wall we could find. The police use the tagging to find out what we were up to just like the gangbangers do. You can tell everything about a 'hood by reading the walls."

— Ruben Alvarez, ex-gang member

"Sometimes when I'm in my car and I see guys walking late at night, I'll stop and give them a ride so they don't get their asses kicked by the police."

—a Hispanic gangbanger

"Some bangers talk about setting up a cop, but when the cops come around they don't do anything."

—a Hispanic gangbanger

"I've even heard them talk about blowing up the police station and say that if the cops come around, they are going to blast them."

—a Hispanic ex-gangbanger

"A Hispanic gangbanger's worst nightmare when dealing with the police is the contact. They hate to be contacted and questioned, whether on foot or on a traffic stop. The police are the enemy unless they need us for something."

—Detective Jack Simington

"Gangs [members] are dumb, but they're not that dumb. They know if they kill a cop that they are going to jail for life. But I know guys who, if the right situation came down, wouldn't hesitate to shoot a cop."

—a Hispanic gangbanger

From time to time there will be a weak member who will inform to the police, but it's rare for a hard-core Hispanic gangbanger to *rata* (rat) to the police. Many times, he will go to prison or even die before he will inform on his homies. To be a snitch to the police is to bring disgrace to himself and his family members. In fact, most bangers will not complain about or testify against rival gangs or individual bangers, preferring to handle the dispute themselves.

Gang officer Scott Gammon says that Hispanic gangbangers have a love/hate relationship with the police. "I believe many of them actually emulate the police due to the fact that they like the power and attention associated with the profession. Many of them also enjoy the attention the police give them, whether it's the officers stopping to talk to them in their neighborhood or when they conduct a high-risk traffic stop. Gangbangers like that because they become the focus of someone's attention.

"Nonetheless, there are times they will verbally and physically intimidate the police on contacts just, as they put it, 'for the fun of it.' Some gang members have a strong hatred toward the police. Obviously, the police are the ones who issue them tickets, follow them around, and take them to jail. Many gang members feel that the cops are the biggest gang in town. They say, 'The cops all wear the same color and drive around and harass people.' With this attitude, the cops are often looked at as the biggest challenge to the gang."

When asked why more police officers aren't getting hurt by gangbangers, Officer Gammon credits increased officer safety, good rapport with gangbangers, and the fact that gangs rarely target the police. "I believe most officers dealing with gangbangers understand the inherent risk and unpredictability that comes with the territory. Therefore, the officer's awareness and degree of safety are at a higher level.

"I have also found that when establishing a personal relationship with gang members, it puts a name and personality to the face and uniform they see. By doing so, I think the banger thinks twice about hurting the officer. Finally, I still see gangbangers, for the most part, targeting only other gangbangers. However, I do know of specific instances where officers have been targeted by gangs."

Louie Lira says that he has no respect for prison corrections officers, parole and probation officers, or police officers. "They are a joke. In the joint, we always have a couple guards on our payroll. On the street, we may not have cops on our payroll, but there are always some who let us do whatever we want to do. When you have a parole officer who is getting ready to violate you, you say 'Hey, mother fucker, you give me a violation and I will kill you.' To gang members who have nothing to lose, these people are a joke."

Lira explains how a gang can bring pressure on an individual in the justice system to do what is right for the gang. "You know, pressure can be a mother fucker. If I'm in prison and doing 25 years to life and know that eventually all my homies are going to be in prison with me, I'll tell them out on the street to talk with that officer and tell him that if he doesn't do what we tell him to do, we are going to deal with his family. We will go and take photographs of his family. What's he going to do? It could be an officer from the police department, the FBI or a corrections officer. What have I got to lose, and my homies got to lose? So, if I can get something out of the system, I do it.

"See, if I go to you and say, 'You know what? I know your wife, your kids, I know where they go, and here is a photograph of them.' And you won't even know who took them. So if your daughter gets shot or kidnapped, you can't blame me for it. I would just say, 'Oh yeah, we had a conversation about it, but we have conversations like this all the time.'

"I've seen this a lot. And the officers say, 'No problem.' I've had officers search me and find cocaine, and they just say, 'OK, see you later, Lou.' What are they going to do? We look at the system and see how we can use it.

"I know a case where a guy got sent to a federal prison. First, let me tell you that I have never, never in my life heard that they put two people in IMU, the hole. You don't do that, because it's against correction's rules. So, this federal guy told this inmate, 'We are going to put you there. There is a person [in the hole] who is going to testify against one of our agents, and we can't have this. So you got to take care of him.' So he goes in there and takes care of it. He gets out, and there is never an investigation or nothing. This guy [the killer] is a member of the Mexican mafia."

VIOLENCE

"I used to know a woman who would sell any kind of weapon you needed. I also used to know where I could get some grenades."

— Albert, ex-Hispanic gangbanger

"Some do drive-bys like going to work. They get up, do the drive-by, and then go on with their day."

—a Hispanic gangbanger

"I did drive-bys just for fun."

—a Hispanic ex-gangbanger

"Some people deal with all their shootings by drinking. They always get drunk before they go out and do it."

—a Hispanic gangbanger

"All of the shootings I've done, I've done sober. I wanted to be wide awake, so I could see the guy's eyes roll over."

—a Hispanic gangbanger

"If a regular citizen is just standing there and gets shot up, so fucking what? He probably wanted to be there, or he probably wanted to be part of a gang. That's why he was there."

—a Hispanic gangbanger

"Happy homes don't send many young people into gangs.

But when homes are not happy or are violent, gang life becomes appealing to them."

—a Hispanic gangbanger

"Sometimes it takes an individual to pump up the gang. When Psycho was alive, everybody would do what he said. Once he died, the whole gang structure went away."

—a Hispanic gangbanger

"It doesn't matter what you have done, whether it is real or imagined. If you are targeted, you might as well think of yourself as dead."

—a Hispanic gangbanger

"In some areas, people think the Hispanic gangs aren't doing anything. But then they're finding all these fucking bodies floating in the river."

—a Hispanic gangbanger

"I'd like to tell some of the mothers that I'm sorry for what I did to their sons, but if I went to them, their other sons would come and say to me, 'Hey, mutha fucker, we been lookin' for you.' So, no, I'll never go and see them."

—a Hispanic ex-gangbanger

"Some cops just do their job; they just talk to you about what is going on. Some are assholes."

—Albert, Hispanic ex-gangbanger

"These days, gangs are fighting mostly over drugs, money, and turf."

—a Hispanic gangbanger

"If drugs were legal, there would still be gangs. Drugs are not the whole reason gangs exist and go to war."

—a Hispanic gangbanger

"Many gangbangers are in fear for their life when they go to prison because of all the different gangs in there. A banger knows he has to be part of a prison gang for protection."

—a Hispanic ex-gangbanger

"Normally, when there is a group of gangbangers, there is one person who holds the guns at his home or a special place. When something happens, a member will request a gun from that person."

—Sandra Davis, ex-gangbanger

"Doing drive-bys can be addictive. It's a rush; it's a habit. I would wonder if my mom was going to be in that house? Will there be officers around the corner? You get addicted to it like it's a drug."

—a Hispanic ex-gangbanger

"I saw many of my homies get wasted by rivals and the police because they were wasted on crack."

—Ruben Alvarez, Hispanic ex-gang member

"The first time I killed someone I cried for about three hours after I got home. Then I thought, hey, it was either him or me. What the fuck am I crying for? So after three hours, I went to sleep and woke up the next day feeling happy. The second time it was a lot easier. I think of it like Vietnam: I needed to do it to survive. And it's like being a cop. If you get into a situation with somebody robbing a bank, what are you going to do? You gotta go home, and so you do what you gotta do. You gotta defend yourself. It's the same with the gang; it's the same way we operate."

—a Hispanic gangbanger

Louie Lira says that in the world of gangs just about anything can justify killing someone. "I'll kill you just because of the way you looked at me. I'll kill you because of the way you were looking at my ol' lady. I'll kill you because you don't respect my set. I'll kill you because I heard from some of my homeboys that you said something bad about me. So, you can be killed for anything, and it can be justified. A lot of it goes back to respect and revenge."

Lira says that Hispanic gangbangers usually pinpoint their targets when they shoot, but there are times when they don't get specific. "Spraying a house doesn't happen in Hispanic gangs a lot, but it might happen every now and then. Sometimes a banger will get real nervous and say, 'Which one is the fuckin' house?' They are having such a rush that they can't see it. They get blind. So, they say, 'Fuck it,' and they start spraying on all the houses. It's like when an officer is pursuing a vehicle. His heart is pounding, and he is having a rush. It's the same with the gangbanger. The same rush. He could even be shooting his own house, because when you mix PCP with cocaine, you don't even know who the fuck you are. If you don't know who you are, how do you know that you aren't killing your own son?"

Lira says that he doesn't respect bangers who shoot wildly. "When I was growing up in the gangs, I hung around with the older gang members so I could learn from them. They told me that you don't go around and shoot houses, because what good does it do? You want to get arrested for shooting a fucking house? You didn't kill it. Even if you don't get arrested, you shouldn't do that. You should walk right up to the person and shoot him five or six times, shoot him right in the head. Other gangs like to shoot up houses, and 95 percent of the time they end up wasting their bullets because they didn't hit anybody. And they feel proud. They go, 'Hey, I did a drive-by, and I shot a house.' So, I say to them, 'Well, you're a big man. So, you like killing houses now? What did you kill? A window?'"

Ex-banger Albert says that in his experience spray-shooting does happen. "A lot of innocent people get shot 'cause I can be standing there with my mom and dad, my little brothers, and one of my friends. Then when a drive-by happens, the bangers see only me and my friend. They don't see the innocent people. They just see the opportunity, and they take it. They got the technology [high-tech weapons], and they don't know how to control the weapons."

As is the case with all street gangs, Hispanic bangers use violence to settle conflict. There is little effort to resolve problems through conversation and various conflict resolution techniques. In far too many cases, the banger is simply doing what he has been taught indirectly to do at home. The home life of many Hispanic gangbangers is one where the parents may themselves be gang affected, the daily family life may be dysfunctional, and it's a place where conflict is handled with violence. If that is all the banger knows, why should anyone be surprised if he carries that out into the street?

CHAPTER 4

SKINHEADS AND OTHER WHITE GANGS

"We must secure the existence for white people and the future for white children."

—A skinhead slogan called "14 Words"

Before I begin, let me give a shameless plug for my book *Skinhead Street Gangs*, a book I humbly believe is the most complete work on the subject. Published by Paladin Press, *Skinhead Street Gangs* has been used as a reference for TV documentaries, news stories, and a couple of movies. The book examines how skins got started in England and in the United States, what they are all about, with whom they affiliate, whom they target, how the police can work them, what to do when they demonstrate in your town, and many other issues. Check it out if you want to expand your knowledge of racist and antiracist skinheads and the white supremacy movement beyond what I present here. Order it from Paladin or check it out on my Web site: http://www.aracnet.com/~lwc123/.

A BRIEF HISTORY

Skinheads can be traced back to the British music culture of the mid-1960s, a time when working-class youths were looking for a different sound from that favored by the hippies and the mods. Although they initially wore their hair long like the other young people, these early skinheads preferred boots and suspenders, as do today's skinheads. They quickly developed a tough reputation because of their frequent fights with the police, soccer players, homosexuals, and hippies. In time, they began shaving their heads to keep from getting their hair pulled and to look different from the other young people.

The country's rising unemployment and increasing immigration began to affect the music scene, and soon skinheads became divided. Some became anti-Semitic, anti-immigration, anti-hippie, and anti-homosexual. This segment of skinheads expressed their philosophy through frequent attacks on immigrants and minorities. The other half of the skinhead movement embraced everything the first group hated.

Skinheads first appeared in the United States in the mid-1980s in many major cities throughout the country, though mostly on the West Coast, in the deep South and in the Midwest. They numbered only a few hundred in the beginning but quickly grew to more than 3,000, a number that, according to such hate-watch groups as Klanwatch and the Southern Poverty Law Center, remains constant today. Although there are not as many skinhead gangbangers as there are in other gangs discussed in this book, skinheads are dangerous beyond their numbers. Today they are in cities large and small everywhere.

THREE TYPES OF SKINHEADS

There are three types of skinheads: SHARP (Skinheads Against Racial Prejudice), traditional, and racist. All three are proud of their uniqueness (although it must be hard to feel unique when they all look the same), and they get quite nasty when they get confused with one of the other types—nasty enough to fight with great violence.

Typically, skinheads shave their heads or cut their hair short, and they wear Doc Marten boots; black Levis, khaki pants, or jeans; suspenders of various colors; white T-shirts; and bomber jackets of various colors. There are variations on the theme, such as medium-length hair while wearing a bomber jacket and boots, or a shaved head but wearing regular street clothing. From 20 feet away, they might all look the same, but upon closer examination one can see tattoos or clothing patches that denote their politics.

All factions claim that they are the true skinheads, and it's not uncommon for the hatred that brews among them to erupt into violence, sometimes deadly. For example, I investigated many cases of assaults, fights, knifings, and shootings between racist and nonracist skinheads, including one incident where a SHARP fatally fired an SKS through the forehead of a racist skinhead. It's important to know that no matter how much each faction says its members are not violent, the potential for it is a strong possibility when they get in each other's faces.

SHARPs

"I get all sorts of shit for bein' a skin, everyone thinkin' I'm a fuckin' bonehead. Nazis are fuckin' scum off the pit of my stomach."

—a SHARP

"There are very few self-admitted SHARPs inside the joint, because most everything is predicated on race. Whites who hang with blacks are looked upon as punks and throwaways. They become targets for the white power inmates. (I'm saying this from my viewpoint as a corrections officer in

Nevada, which is similar to California. I have been told that the prisons in the Midwest accept mixed-race gangs."

—Corrections Sergeant Bill Valentine

"I'm a SHARP, and I'm a real skinhead, not a bonehead, one of those closed-minded scumbags who call themselves a skin. I don't like black trash, and I don't like white trash or any other trash. My belief is to stay true to yourself and don't let anyone bring you down. Hard work is good for you. I've lived on the East Coast almost all my 18 years."

—a SHARP

SHARPs stand for just about everything that racist skinheads oppose. Although they tell the media that they are nonviolent, their past deeds make it clear that they will clash with anyone they oppose. SHARPs are probably the most well-known of the antiracist factions, though there are other groups with names (usually acronyms), as well as groups that don't have names but share the same philosophy.

Antiracists claim to be the original skinheads, those that started in England, and detest being identified as racist. Of course, this confusion will continue as both racists and antiracists refuse to change their nearly identical look.

Their Web sites, their literature, and their interviews with the press are aimed at convincing people that they are the "good skinheads." Don't believe it. While there are those antiracists who are law-abiding, there are others who are criminal and act out as gangs do.

Traditionalists

"Here's a little message to the skinheads that think that just because they are SHARPs or white power that they are true skinheads. Well, you know what? You are wrong. Being a skinhead isn't about being in some organization, hell-bent on destroying those opposing. Being a skinhead is about standing up for what you believe. In my opinion, if you don't have enough confidence to be an independent skinhead for a while, you have no business being a skinhead. I don't have a problem with anybody unless you try to fuck with me. And if you fuck with me, I don't care what your race, religion, or ethnic background, you should prepare to take a boot to the head. Keep your politics to yourself. I have been a skinhead for about six years; for four of them I was a SHARP, and I regret every moment of it."

—an independent traditional skinhead

Traditional skinheads are similar to SHARPs. They are both skins who have no official political or racial beliefs, though most oppose and dislike Nazi and racist skins. SHARPs and traditionalists share a fondness for the same kind of music, "ska" music, which is light, jazzy, and somewhat like reggae.

Many racist and antiracist skinheads claim to be traditionalists when stopped by the police. In their minds, they think that if they don't claim an affiliation with the more notorious skins, the police will hassle them less.

Racist Skinheads

"It is really scary to think how easy it is to hate."

—an ex-racist skinhead

"I believe that all niggers should burn along with all the rest of these goddamn Jewish mother fuckers. White Power!"

—a racist skinhead

"Do the world a favor and send the niggers back to Africa, then nuke Africa. HEIL HITLER, and keep fighting for our future."

—a racist skinhead

"Senseless violence is my favorite game.
If everyone dies, I am not to blame.
Burn their smelling corpses into the ground.
I will make sure nobody is to be found."

—from a song by Ken Death, a racist skinhead who is now serving time for the murder of a black man

"We want our own land where we can celebrate our white culture."

—a racist skinhead

"The minorities really got it in for us. They're really jealous of us. The government really sets them towards us. They wanna get rid of the real Americans. They wanna really stick it to us, give us the shaft; kick us out of jobs."

—a racist skinhead

"We are a group of young people of the extreme right. We are called [name deleted], and we are violent. We fight the drug addicts, vagrants, and prostitutes. We are not racists, but we believe that each race ought to stay in its place. We are not copies of the German skinheads. We don't have to read Hitler to love our country. We simply apply his ideas to our society."

—a racist skinhead

"Jesus sent me. The man with the bloody hands asked me to give you a personal fucking message: God hates Niggers. You won't see one fucking Negro in heaven. Or any of you darkie-loving, gook-fucking SHARP whores either. Mark 13:4: 'And quoth the Lord, "Goddamn, these jungle bunnies smell! And the mountains shook, and donkeys pissed Jell-O."'"

—a racist skin

"Hitler was most definitely the greatest man of our time. He offered us the only realistic chance at saving our race and

Is there any doubt about which type of skinhead owns this truck?

faith from organized world Jewry. It is my belief that we boneheads [racist skinheads] offer the only reasonable chance for our children to grow up without having to worry about being gang-raped by a bunch of drug-soaked, savage black animals."

—a racist skin

The racists are the skinheads most people think of and the ones that get most of the press. They blame other races for all that is wrong in America and show their rage and hatred in acts of violence against people of other races, political beliefs, religions, sexual preferences, and virtually everyone in the government.

RESPECT

It has been my experience that most skinheads, especially the racist variety, are losers. They do poorly in school, their

The mind-set of these racist skinheads can be seen in their Nazi salute, their shaved heads, the Confederate flag that depicts their belief in the ways of the Old South, the American flag that symbolizes their desire for a white-controlled America, and the bayonet poised to back up their beliefs.

social skills are nil, and their self-esteem is on the skids. Although their involvement in a skinhead gang doesn't do much to improve their social skills, it does give their self-esteem a boost. They are somebody, a member of a group that gets its power from their philosophy, goals, numbers, and the color of their skin. Whereas no one gave them respect before, now when they wear their regalia—boots, khaki pants, suspenders, shaved heads, and tattoos—and stomp along the streets in mob formation, people get out of their way. The respect they garner from this, though negative, gives them the self-esteem they never had before.

My experience with antiracist skins has been basically the same. Many of them come from the streets and have discovered that by becoming a member of a group opposed to racism they get respect from their fellow skins and sometimes from the naive media. They also get negative respect by virtue of their appearance, a look that is nearly the same as that of the racist skinheads. Their shaved heads and all their regalia frighten the general populace, who see all skinheads, no matter what their politics, as thugs.

Bill Ottaway is an ex-racist skinhead who says his early life is fairly typical of other skins. "Most skins have, at one point, been deeply hurt, whether it was a family situation or a social situation, such as being picked on at school. My personal experience was that I was tormented throughout school and that, coupled with family problems, I was left in a situation where I was searching for something I could be part of, such as a member of a gang. I was looking for respect among my peers, and I found that skins respect each other just because of racial heritage. I am Irish/English, and that simple bloodline allowed me to enter a blood bond with others who were searching for respect.

"Another aspect of respect that is important to skins is that of societal respect. Skins look at today's society as a cesspool, and they believe that they have the answer to the problem. We choose violence because many times that is the only thing that people will respect, though the respect is out of fear."

REPUTATION

Skins have a reputation to uphold, that of being tough and hard. When racist skinheads get offended by a minority that happens to be in their midst, they feel it's their duty to strike out verbally and physically. When a racist skinhead happens to be in the area of a group of nonracist skins, the latter has a reputation to uphold by striking out against the racists. Skinheads on both sides enjoy the reputation they have and bask in the reactions they get from people.

Bill Ottaway says this about the importance of reputation: "Reputation is important because that is what preceded us when I was running with the skins. When people saw my bald head, they immediately knew what I stood for and what I was willing to do to defend my beliefs. Skins wear their heritage as a badge of honor. My flight jacket was covered with Irish flags, English flags and, of course, Nazi historical pieces. The most important was the swastika and also the Iron Cross. Many times our reputation invoked fear in people; sometimes it invoked anger. People would stare but rarely say anything. Minorities especially would stay away from us."

REVENGE

Like other street gangs, skinheads seek revenge when they feel that they have been wronged. People who snitch on them and people who are witnesses against them to the police are often fair game for retaliation. And since there is a continuous rivalry between racist and antiracist skins, there is virtually a built-in revenge clause when one side in some way offends the other side. Revenge is important to both of them because they must uphold their reputation.

Bill Ottaway says that revenge is integral to what skinheads are about. "We searched for revenge on a society that has walked away from traditional values and accepted what we thought to be degenerate values. Nazi skinheads are a group that does not compromise. We don't accept the state that the world is in, but rather look to the thousands of years before us that created a utopian society of racial purity and genetic uniformity. Each act of violence or propaganda is an act of revenge on a group of people who are wallowing in self-pity and weak-minded behavior."

I investigated many cases of skinheads assaulting mixed-race couples. In a way, these violent acts are a way of retaliating against a violation they see perpetrated by other whites. Miscegenation (mixing of the races), they say, muddies the gene pool. This angers them, so they strike out against the white half of the relationship, and, of course, they strike out at the minority half, too.

I also investigated incidents of one skinhead faction striking back against another faction. Acts of retaliation took the form of drive-by shootings, knifings, and street rumbles. Although violence between opposing skinhead factions was at times intense, it never came near the violence that we see committed by other gangs, such as when Bloods and Crips clash. Although today skinhead violence is low, there is still an intense hatred between the racists and antiracists. If one side is wronged in some fashion by the other side, it's almost guaranteed that there will be an act of revenge.

BELONGING AND IDENTITY

"Being a skinhead is about always fighting for what you believe is right and backing up a skin even when you know he or she is wrong. It's about being the first to open a beer at a party and the last to leave. It's about thinking for yourself and knowing that nobody is better than you. It's about listening to street music when others are listening to the crap on the charts. And, as has been said many times before, being a skinhead is a way of life, one that lives on in your heart long after you've hung up your boots and braces."

—a racist skinhead

"I may not be completely for white power, but I'm not

against it. I'm not a fence-sitter. I used to be white power, but I started being traditional. I'm starting to see that my opinion is my own, and fuck everyone who opposes. I turn on the television, and all it is are old people rapping and everyone is trying to be a nigger. Fuck that! I can't remember the last time I saw a white kid that actually dressed like they were white. It pisses me off. You don't have to be a nigger like the spics and gooks and scum like such. If I ever see a faggot skinhead, I'll stomp his ass. How can anyone be a skinhead and a cock-sucking, ass-banging, AIDS-infested, rainbow-flag-waving queer? Die fags, die gooks and mud people of all walks of the Earth. White pride."

—a female racist skinhead

"Being a skinhead is to swear to love your race and push it into the forefront. We spent our time pushing our beliefs to others in order to gain more and more followers. Skins are very conservative. They do not believe in abortion, homosexuality, drugs, or other immoral behavior. This was the most attractive portion of the life because I believed that the entire decline of America was directly attributable to the moral state of our nation. The biggest thing about being a neo-Nazi skinhead was the danger. A skinhead's beliefs are considered radical because of the emphasis on racial differences. Because of this skins are regularly attacked."

—an ex-racist skinhead

"The sense of belonging was invaluable. We stuck together like brothers, rarely going out alone. That sense of belonging was crucial. To know that there are 10 to 20 guys that are willing to die for me at any given moment—that is a powerful feeling; a feeling that takes all the fear out of you."

—Bill Ottaway, ex-racist skinhead

"The average skin just wants to live, work, and fight."

— a racist skinhead

**"We're all skinheads we stand proud,
We're working class and shout it out loud,
We love our oi! that's what we live for,
Can't get enough we always want more . . .
The Pride, the pride."
—from a poem or song, unknown author**

"There are men, and there are beasts. Men and women of the Aryan race are men. If you are not of the Aryan race, then you are a beast."

—a racist skinhead

"It's all about racial pride and nationalistic pride."
—a racist skinhead

"No other cult offers the same sense of belonging, of

brotherhood, that skinheads offer each other across the globe. And that's why we'll still be hanging about on street corners in 25 years."

—an antiracist skinhead

"The movement can have a powerful effect on impressionable young people, so much so that they will even kill their parents."

—Brian Levin of the Southern Poverty Law Center

"Young men and women join out of a need to be accepted. Unlike other gangs, there is only one requirement to join a racist skinhead gang—Aryan heritage, whether it's Irish, English, German, or Scandinavian. It doesn't matter. It is something white kids can identify with. Fighting ability and appearance come later. Skins will accept a white man and change him later."

—a racist skinhead

"Skinheads believe in 'jumping out,' as opposed to many black gangs that believe in 'jumping in.' That means that if you leave then they will hunt you down and punish you. To leave is treason to skinheads. I still have skins who call and harass me. I'm not really afraid for me, but I worry about my family at times."

—an ex-racist skinhead

"Skinheads who [are] wounded or killed become an inspiration to others."

—a racist skinhead

"When I joined the skins and shaved my head, I felt powerful. I had a solid identity, I felt confident, and I was ready for anything."

—a female skinhead

This illustration depicts cartoon caricatures of various racial and ethnic groups who racist skinheads believe are taking over America.

"I'm a working-class kid from an upper-class district in the same situation. People are ignorant and think that all skins are those racist bonehead mother fuckers. I'm not a SHARP, but I'm being forced to become one for the reason that there are too many fucking boneheads out there, and I want to do something about it. The skinhead culture has been tainted by racism, and it'll never be the same. I am disgusted by all you traitors who call yourselves skinheads. Being a skinhead is about being white, working class, and not bending over and taking a bunch of shit from weak-ass liberal sheep. Why can't you just let it alone? Skinhead means white power."

—from a somewhat confused skinhead

Belonging to the group is what being a skinhead is all about. Membership gives strength, power, love, a sense of family, and a place to be. You can see it from the way the skinheads "walk hard" together, hold themselves, posture, talk loudly and animatedly, and virtually burst with the power they get from being in a group where everyone thinks the same way. On the other hand, when you see them out and about by themselves, they are usually less brazen. They don't walk as hard as they do when in a group; in fact, many times they seem a little nervous, their eyes darting about like a frightened deer in the forest.

Racist skinheads are racially motivated, as opposed to being territorial or profit motivated like other ethnic gangs. The racists' extreme hatred for all people who are different gives them a sense of brotherhood with others who are also white and filled with hatred. They may not have money, education, or a real family, but they have a white pigmentation, which gives them power and a strong sense of belonging.

My psychology 101 take on the racist variety of skinheads is that the group dynamic appeals to those who are afraid of the world around them. Their philosophy and hate give them something to believe in, yet their paranoia causes them to see

Jew Dwarfs!
There is an oven in YOUR future!

Racist skinheads hate Jewish people.

everyone, especially every organization with an affiliation with the government (which they call ZOG, Zionist Occupational Government), as being out to get them.

The antiracist skins may not have the paranoia about Jewish agents from the ZOG lurking behind every bush, but they do see a Nazi lurking there. It's this paranoia that provides them with their collective thought, their sense of "us versus them." They feel a sense of pride about their claim to be the true skinheads, and they feel a sense of bravado as they huddle and talk of doing battle against the racists.

Skinheads who are forced to join a gang or those who join out of a need to survive are less likely to have the same sense of belonging as those who have grown up with racist beliefs. There are those, however, who grow into the gang and all that it stands for and, as a result, are more than willing to fight hard. As ex-skinhead Bill Ottaway says, "The one who is forced will never fully believe in what he is doing. He will simply fight for something that is not instilled in him, but will fight out of a fear of rejection. The one who wants to join will fight for a belief that he is willing to die for."

Occasionally, there are skinheads who will switch allegiance. A person will be a racist for a while and then will reappear on the scene as an antiracist. I recall one skinhead who switched every few weeks and carried sew-on patches and paperwork in his pockets from both factions. In his case, he enjoyed the media attention and would switch to whichever side was getting the most press.

PHILOSOPHY

More than the other gangs discussed in this book, skinheads are about their philosophy. Here is how they view the world.

Racist Skinheads

"We [racists skinheads] are the white blood cells of the white race. When the body has a sickness the white cells come out and attack it. That's what skinheads are: we are a natural instinctual reaction of the white race."

—a racist skinhead

"I think Hitler was somewhat liberal. I would have been more ruthless."

—Tom Metzger, leader of White Aryan Resistance (WAR)

"White supremacy philosophy in the joint runs a broad spectrum from dabblers on up to violent racists. A large majority of whites have SWP [Supreme White Power] type ink [tattoos]; of these, most are down for the white race and will hang tough with others during times of racial strife. But some of the dabblers will check into protective custody."

—Sergeant Bill Valentine

"The niggers are getting all the best jobs, all the advancement. The goddamn spics are taking our jobs and the food off our table."

—a racist skinhead

"We're pro-majority, pro-working man, pro-youth, and pro-America. The Nationalists' goal is a nation without minority power."

—Richard Barrett, 50, attorney and skinhead advocate

"We're going to fight to take our country back from the communists and gays and minorities."

—a racist skinhead

"Skins want the complete separation of the races; they will accept nothing less. They believe that most of the evil in the country is because of multiculturalism. Skins want the return of the Aryan empire. They want a return to a time when the white man controlled this country. This philosophy is their passion."

—an ex-racist skinhead

Whenever I asked young racist skinheads or middle-aged white supremacists whom they hated, they always answered quickly with "the Jews." One skinhead gave the following explanation.

"Love and hate go hand in hand. If you love your family, then it's a natural instinct to hate that which would want to threaten your family. So because the parasitical race of Jews [is] a direct threat to the white race, whom we love dearly, we therefore hate them for their actions directed against us. If they want to stay in Israel and leech off the Palestinians, then that's their problem. But instead they want to live in America and be parasites off society and control the mass media and deliberately lie about anyone who is proud to be white. It's OK to be black and proud or Jewish and proud of it. But if you're white and proud, you're a bigot."

In addition to their racist philosophy, white supremacist skinheads have strong beliefs about politics and what is going on in the country. Some are quite knowledgeable about what is going on in their world, though many times their thoughts are askew on what is reality. Some are also knowledgeable about history, especially Nazi history, and they often possess a fine collection of literature on the subject. But, again, their take on what really happened during those horrific years is skewed from the misinformation they have received in modern-day, white supremacy literature, especially material written by revisionists.

Antiracist Skinheads

Here are some quotes from a group calling themselves Red and Anarchist Skinheads (RASH), who say they are not racist but that their purpose is to fight for the working class. RASH appears to be larger in Europe than in the United States; I believe there are just a few on the East Coast. I am putting their quotes here because the language and the content are quite typical of what I have heard so many times from antiracist skinheads. While some of it is nonsensical, and phrased awkwardly (I've tried to tidy the spelling and gram-

A racist skinhead named BASH marked his name and a swastika on a wall. Later, an antiracist skinhead drew a diagonal line through the swastika.

matical errors), I think it will give you a sense of where they are coming from philosophically.

First, here are some of their goals:

- To combat, physically and politically, the existence of far-right ideas in the skinhead scene
- To win back the good name of our subculture from the boneheads and racists
- To articulate the connection between the young, working-class, multiracial skinhead subculture and left-wing ideas
- To organize for the physical self-defense of left-wing skinheads from attack by all those who declare themselves our enemies
- To participate as an active, organized force of antiracist skinheads in the radical left and antifascist movements
- To make sure our vision of the antifascist radical left (working-class, multiracial, street-based, and militant) continues to exist

RASH members in North America are proud of their culture, heritage, and the sacrifices made by U.S. workers (don't think too many factory owners fought fascism in the trenches of Europe) have made toward our freedom. To us, the American rebel worker is quintessential America, and we know that we have more in common with workers of any other country than our bosses, politicians, cops, etc., and that's where our loyalty lies—not to our political or economic masters. We believe in democracy (both political and economic), freedom, and justice, and hate capitalism and fascism.

"We've all gotten a raw deal from the beginning. We go to work every day, try to do right, and are repaid with starvation wages. There are now more prisons, no health care, and no education beyond high school for most of us. RASH skins believe that capitalism has turned into a hellish nightmare.

"This planet offers bountiful resources, enough for all of us to live comfortably and be more able to do the things in life that really matter (instead of wasting our lives on cheap beer and overtime). There is only one reason why this isn't the case. Ten percent of the earth's population controls 90 percent or more of the earth's resources. We believe that it is the historic mission of the working class to struggle against, and eventually destroy, the parasites who gorge themselves on luxury at the expense of those of us who produce all of the world's wealth. To put it simply, 'Them that works not shall not eat!'"

But this is what one racist skinhead organization says about RASH and SHARP. "The age-old Jewish MO [modus operandi] is divide and conquer. The Jews fully realize that the most dangerous thing to happen is the skinhead movement, simply because of their dedication to action. So the Jews cleverly came up with something to wreck this potential. In 1990 the ADL [Anti-Defamation League] in San Francisco went to the skinhead capital of the world, Portland Oregon, and sought out lowlife punks. They paid these two punks to shave their Mohawks and to dress and look like skinheads, but to be antiracist. It wasn't real hard to find punks who were pissed off at skinheads, since a lot of punks had gotten beat up for being freaks. So Skinheads Against Racial Prejudice was formed. That's called an oxymoron.

"Basically the concept is to have the skinheads fighting each other, therefore being too busy to contemplate action against the real masters of hate, the filthy kikes. RASH is just more wanna-be skinheads. And you also now have GAS [Gay Aryan Skinheads], a bunch of faggots, so they say. I don't personally believe it's true. I think it's just a paid Jewish group to disrupt the concept of skinheads, to make it seem like a joke. No known faggot would ever show up at a white power rally or even associate with anyone willing to die for the white family. These faggots have nothing to do with white power, no more than these other fakes have anything to do with white power. The only common denominator they have with us is a boot party. The only good faggot is a dead faggot. Period. Either way, none of these wanna-be skinhead groups amount to anything."

Whatever the skinhead faction, there are those who are zealots and willing to do whatever it takes to support their philosophy. Recent history has shown us repeatedly that some racist skinheads are more than willing to fight and kill for their philosophy. Many who are antiracist and of the traditionalist faction also get so caught up in what they believe that they are willing to fight and kill for it. Skinheads from all factions deny their willingness to use violence, but I have found the thinking process of all the groups, as it concerns rivals, to be no different than that between Bloods and Crips.

On the other hand, there are skinheads in both factions who have no philosophy at all. They are simply along for the ride—the fun, the excitement, the attention, the sense of belonging. They either don't care about a philosophy or they lack the intelligence to form one.

This drawing shows a Klan member and a neo-Nazi skinhead hanging an antiracist skinhead.

Tattoos

Tattoos give a clear indication of where a skinhead's mind is. Antiracists have a few tattoos that designate their philosophy; racist skins have many.

Antiracist Tattoos

Antiracists commonly have tattoos that are similar to those of punk rockers—skulls, cobwebs, music symbols, anything that depicts gore. In fact, so much so that they are often confused with Satanists. They may very well be involved in Satanic activity, but it's not an automatic indicator. Here are a few of the tattoos that depict their antiracist philosophy:

- A swastika with a diagonal line through it
- The word Hate with a diagonal line through it
- The acronym SHARP
- The letter A (anarchy) sometimes seen on racist skinheads
- Any tattoo that indicates racial harmony
- For SHARPs, often a skinhead on a cross

Racist Tattoos

Racist skins also wear lots of tattoos that are similar to punk rockers' and Satanists'. The following are a few tattoos that indicate their racist philosophy:

- Swastikas
- The letters AB (Aryan Brotherhood)
- The numbers 666 (Aryan Brotherhood)
- The letters SS, sometimes called lightning bolts (The SS was Hitler's storm trooper organization.)
- Any art that depicts the Viking culture, such as horned helmets, muscular Viking warriors, Viking women, or axes
- The letters SWP, for Supreme White Power (Although this is a group in some prisons, skins on the street wear the tattoo as an indicator of their philosophy.)

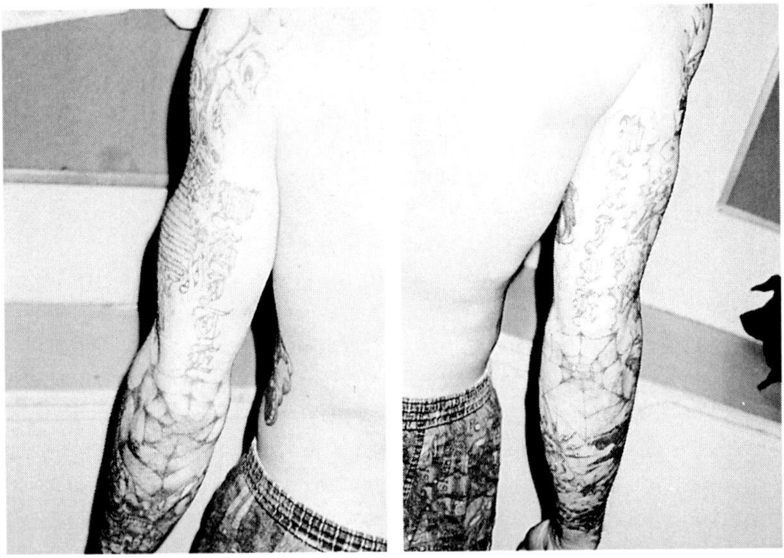

"White" on the left arm and "Pride" on the right arm with other tattoos that depict cobwebs and skulls are typically found on racist skinheads.

- The words White Power
- The words White Pride
- The letters HH (Heil Hitler)
- German Iron Cross
- American flag
- Aryan Nations symbol
- Crossed axes and crossed hammers
- Celtic cross

THEY THINK IN THE NOW

"I can't believe someone can die from just a couple hits with a 2x4."

—a racist skinhead to me a few hours after the beating death of another racist skinhead

"It wasn't a planned thing. I walked through town with my gun in my waist, saw the black guy, and thought he didn't belong where he was at. I thought how easy it would be to take him out right there. Didn't seem like much to me."

—a racist skinhead after he had
shot and killed a black man

"In a war, anybody wearing the enemy's uniform [meaning that they are a minority] should be taken out."

—a racist killer skinhead

Many skinheads are kids and, as such, live for the moment with little or no thought to the future or the consequences of their actions. They see a target, and they go after it. I can give many examples of spur-of-the moment acts of violence by racists and antiracists who had given their deeds no more thought than "let's attack that guy."

An Ethiopian immigrant was brutally beaten to death moments after six skinheads, three male and three female, parked next to a car containing three Ethiopians on a quiet, residential street in my city. There was a short exchange of words between the passengers in the cars, and then the skins leaped from theirs and chased the immigrants. Two of the Ethiopians escaped but one was caught and beaten to death with a baseball bat. There was no planning or thought given to the horrific act.

On another occasion, an antiracist skinhead walked into a convenience store and saw a female he believed was a racist skinhead. Without hesitation, he pulled a hammer from under his coat and smashed her in the head. He was subsequently caught and given 14 months in prison for the attack. It turned out that the young girl, who was severely injured, had no skinhead ties whatsoever.

This lack of planning on their part makes it difficult to anticipate what they are going to do. The police might get some warning of a demonstration or a march, but it's difficult to get good intelligence about an impending assault or any other crime, since to them the word *impending* usually means one minute from the present. So, if they don't know they are going to do something before it happens, the police sure won't have a clue.

VIOLENCE

"Line them up against the wall,
Shoot them, watch them die.
I love to hear the agony.
They vomit, scream, and cry."

—song by Ken Death

"I like breaking arms and legs
Snapping spines and wringing necks
Now I'll knife you in the back
Kick your bones until they crack
(chorus) Evil, evil, evil, evil
Evil, evil, evil, evil
Evil, evil, evil, evil
Evil, evil, evil, evil
Jump up and down upon your head
Kick you around 'til you're dead
Fill your body full of lead
See the roads turn to red."

—song by 4 Skins

"We won't be beaten in an attack, fuck with us and get hit with a bat
You may be big, but you're not too tough
Drink and fight, can't get enough
Walking down the street, looking for a fight
You know we will come out on top, that's right
(chorus) We will not . . .
Give in to you
We will not . . .
Give in to you."

—song by The Paxton Boys

"To a skinhead, hurting or killing someone is a means to an end. Beating 10, 20, or 100 minorities is a stepping-stone toward the ultimate prize of racial superiority. The opposite is in fact true: it simply angers minorities and incites further hostility. This once again plays into skins' hands because they love confrontation."

—an ex-racist skinhead

"I would just like to say that all you sad, fucking, simple-minded, mother-fucking, racist fuckheads need shooting."

—a SHARP

"Fuck the niggers. I will kill all of you monkeys."

—a racist skinhead

"The biggest attack actually comes from within our own race. SHARPs are about 60 percent of the fights I was in as a skinhead. Skinheads are the most violent group I have ever been in contact with. We fought gangs and other groups, but our determination was what led us and supercharged us. We would routinely look for fights. We used baseball bats, pipes, clubs, and bottles. I had no regard for human life. I was hate. If a person looked at me wrong, I would walk up to him and pound him. I beat people unmercifully. There were nights that I would end up running from the police because I had bashed some guys up with my tire iron."

—an ex-racist skinhead

"I once beat up a black guy because he looked at a girl that was hanging out with us. We routinely beat up race mixers and gays and any other person who we thought deserved it. I had friends that were in jail for malicious maiming, assault, and even murder."

—an ex-racist skinhead

"I look at beating up fags as a way of cleaning up the

streets. I don't see it as wrong. Fuck those fucking people; they're nothing. They fucking breathe my air."

—a racist skinhead

"Violence is a means to an end."

—a racist skinhead

"We meet violence with violence. If violence comes towards us, we'll be there to defend ourselves because we don't run; we won't back down."

—a racist skinhead

"Amid shouts of 'you're gonna die,' over a dozen members of the group invaded the party, wielding knives, chains, pipes, an ax handle, and a broomstick, according to police and media reports. The skinheads directed most of their rage at a 22-year-old, the young man who had originally ousted them from the party. After he was knocked to the ground, the leader of the group—a longtime skinhead who had moved to the area from the Midwest after serving jail time for rape and robbery—straddled the victim's beaten body and stabbed him nine times, according to police. The young man died in the arms of his fiancée."

—from a news account of an East Coast skinhead incident

"A gang of skinheads confronted minorities hanging out on the city's fishing piers and asked if they believed in white power. When a Native American man tried to flee their approach, the thugs chased him down, and one of the group stabbed him 27 times in what officers called a 'particularly frenzied' attack."

—from a news account of a
skinhead incident on the West Coast

These crimes—and there are many, many more just like

Racist skinheads demonstrate in front of a government building.

them—show the usual elements of skinhead-related violence. The racist gangbangers operate in well-armed packs, targeting Jews, blacks, gays, and other minorities. Even homeless people have been victimized by them, sometimes fatally. Although skinheads are few in number, their rage and violent acts make up for it. Psychologists say their actions are an outgrowth of the anger and alienation they feel. Whatever the reasons, when they strike, they do so hard and explosively, an approach typical of most racially motivated violence.

Antiracist skinheads, for the most part, have a venomous hatred for the boneheads. One day, they carry picket signs and parade back and forth in front of a skinhead's house or workplace, and then the next day they physically attack someone they think is a racist skin.

DENIAL

"Many skins deny their involvement to make their day easier. When people think of Nazi Germany, they think of mass extermination. Skins think of Nazi Germany as the physical shape of racial pride and nationalistic attitude. Many times, skins are more effective if they are not noticed."

—Bill Ottaway, ex-racist skinhead

Racist skinheads often deny who they are by claiming to be a SHARP skinhead. As mentioned earlier, many of them believe that claiming to be an antiracist skinhead will get them less attention from the police.

Antiracists skinheads often claim to not be affiliated with any skinhead faction. It can be quite amusing to have one stand before you, decked out in all the skin regalia—flight jacket, boots, suspenders, and with shaved head—and deny his involvement.

THE POLICE

> DENVER—After a series of fatal shootings, high-speed chases, running gun battles, and death threats involving violent young white supremacists, authorities here put the city on what amounted to a skinhead alert Thursday.
>
> As police fanned out across a 20-block portion of west Denver in search of a young white male who had fired on an officer Thursday morning, authorities launched a cooperative effort with the FBI, the Drug Enforcement Administration, and the Bureau of

Alcohol, Tobacco, and Firearms to determine whether recent incidents were part of a skinhead uprising or mere coincidence.

The trouble started a week ago when 11-year police veteran Bruce Vander Jagt was shot and killed after a high-speed chase with a skinhead who ultimately committed suicide with the slain officer's handgun.

On Tuesday, a dead pig was dumped in the parking lot of the slain officer's station house. Etched on the side of the carcass was Vander Jagt's name. On its belly, someone had carved the image of a police badge around the word "pig."

—from a news item in the
Los Angeles Times by Louis Sahagun

"These younger skins really see the cops as the enemy. It is really seen to be a badge of honor to cap [kill] a cop."

—an ex-skinhead

"Nazi skinheads don't see the police as the enemy; they won't attack them. I've always looked at police officers as the average white guy who wants to live in a safe America, free from violence. We never go after the police and, in fact, we always show them respect."

—a racist skinhead

TO PROTECT AND SERVE THE ZIONIST INTERNATIONAL

"You Boys in blue,
Whoever the Jew . . .
Think you're making things safe.
They throw you bones,
And protect their vile skins . . .

Spitting on your own kinsmen,
Again and again.
Now, there's WAR in the air,
Because we've had enough . . .
And real damn soon,
It's gonna get rough!
Righteous WHITE anger,
Is what you will feel . . .
As we smash the system,
With fire and steel!
The Jew masters we'll pile,
On Huge smoking pyres . . .
YOUR ASS IS OURS."

—a song or possibly a poem by an anonymous skinhead

"A lot of skins have a lot of respect for the police. We feel like they are on our side by putting scum in jail. Police on the other hand, really dislike us; they look at us like we're punks. They think we are on drugs and that we vandalize. But being a skinhead means no drugs and respect for women and respect for others."

—a racist skinhead

During the years I worked skinheads and white supremacists in general, I was hated, liked, targeted for death, and made special in their minds because I was the media spokesperson for the gang unit. Some of them snitched to me; some lied; some refused to say a word. All this led to the conclusion in my mind that there are no absolutes when dealing with them as a police officer. It's important to keep in mind that most skinheads are young, spontaneous, violent, angry, and cowardly—a bad mix in which to place any amount of trust or your personal safety.

The racist skinheads see the police as part of ZOG, that

is, bowing to the minorities and oppressing hard-working whites. The uniform symbolizes everything that they are angry about. I don't find it surprising at all that an officer was killed recently and another one was sniped at by racist skinheads. What amazes me is that it hasn't happened before.

Antiracist skinheads feel they have a right to attack anyone whose philosophy is different from theirs, which means the police can be a thorn in their paw by interrupting their objectives and arresting them. They see the police as fascists and Nazi racists. Since the police are part of the problem, the antiracists won't hesitate to attack. They did in Portland, Oregon—attacking officers with thrown bricks and bottles.

Free advice: if you work in law enforcement or any other part of the justice system, consider using your work address on your vehicle registration, driver's license, and personal checks, and keep your name and number out of the phone book. Always be cautious of your surroundings as you walk and drive on and off the job.

Is this being paranoid? Nope. My family was followed, my kids were watched in high school, I was followed off duty, I was sent hate literature, my name was chanted during street demonstrations, and even my library card was tampered with in the library's computer system. Fortunately, my agency installed an alarm in my home, allowed me to take a radio home each day, and had the neighborhood beat car give my house a little extra patrol. Of course, I had my two buddies with me inside my home: my Glock 9mm and my SKS.

Even with all the precautions, it's important to keep in mind that if someone really wants a piece of you, it's not that hard to find where you live.

Stay alert.

A PARTING QUOTE

"Right now there are a lot of old-school skins from the

Racists light a swastika to celebrate their beliefs.

1980s getting out of the movement, and there are a lot of 'fresh cuts' getting in. This changes the movement a lot. The old school has really kept to themselves the last five to ten years, but the fresh cuts are ready to make a name for themselves. They are being groomed right now by older skins, and I would say that in three years there will be a revival in the Nazi movement. Their feelings on violence have not changed at all. To sum it up, skins use the expression 'You can't cure cancer with aspirin.' This means that you will not overthrow this society with fistfights.

"Therefore, I believe that a lot of bombings and other terrorist acts will take place in the future from skinhead groups."

—Bill Ottaway, ex-racist skinhead

MISCELLANEOUS WHITE GANGS

When most people think of white gangs, they usually think about skinheads. But there are more and more white youth getting involved in gangs that have nothing to do with white supremacy or antiracist philosophies. We began seeing them in Portland in 1990, in what appeared to be a response to all the media attention the other gangs were getting virtually every night on the five o'clock news. Some of these gangs were short-lived, whereas others stayed around for a year or more.

Back then, most white gangs started out as graffiti gangs, usually called "crews," as in paint crew. They formed simply to mark, or "tag," their crew's name and their individual street monikers on walls, fences, and street signs. Conflicts arose quickly when one tagging crew would tag over another crew's graffiti, an act considered a major diss. Some tagging crews disbanded when violence broke out, but others graduated into violent gangs, no longer existing solely to mark up walls.

Today, white gangs are still here. The California Department of Justice estimates there could be as many as 5,000 white gang members in California. And that's just California. Everywhere, now, white gangs form to emulate established gangs, usually the black gangs, though they can be found running with Hispanic and Southeast Asian gangs. Like young people in all ethnic gangs, white youths perceive some kind of glamor in the lifestyle and believe that if they belong to a gang they will gain power and respect.

Some white gangbangers are influenced by today's fashions. Baggy pants and oversized shirts, typical of gang attire, are currently fashionable in the teenage clothing industry. Gangster music, which depicts musicians wearing gang-style clothing, drinking from 40-ounce beer bottles, cruising in low-rider cars, hanging out on street corners, walking tough, displaying firearms under shirts, and clashing with rivals, is all over television in the form of music videos. Wearing gang-style clothing and watching irresponsible entertainment are all it takes for some impressionable young people to take that extra step into gangs.

Mike Douthit, who prefers to be called Hellraiser, is white and belongs to a gang of mixed-race gangbangers. He says he became involved in gangs to be part of something and to get the stability he wasn't getting from his home life. "I joined because I was angry at the world and at society in general," he says. "I justified everything I did because of the way I was treated at home and by society. I believed that if people weren't going to respect me or give me what I felt I deserved, then I was going to take it. If that meant killing . . . oh well, I guess you die."

REPUTATION, RESPECT, AND REVENGE

As with all gangs, reputation is paramount among white gangbangers. "If you want to be known to other gangbangers," Hellraiser says, "you got to have a rep. Without it, you are nobody. Our symbols and colors make us known throughout the streets, and they let our rivals and everyone else know what our intentions are. A reputation as a known killer and being very easy to anger earned me my nickname. It's also a boost to your rep if you have been shot or locked up.

"Respect to a gangbanger is as important as his reputation. Without it, he is nobody. The respect he gets is determined by how much pain he inflicts and the type of crimes he commits. It's tied into his rep. Bangers love the attention they get from people and from the media because they get more respect from

Reputation, respect, and revenge are all-important to white gangbangers.

it and a better reputation. In the mind of a gangbanger, hurting or killing someone is justified by the lack of respect and how a banger is treated by society.

"Revenge is very important, almost as much as respect and reputation. If a gangbanger feels someone is dissing him or has hurt someone he cares about, the gangbanger must seek revenge. If he doesn't, then he is looked down on by his set as being weak. The shootings I've been involved in, I was just thinking about revenge. I wanted to make sure that the person who disrespected me was not able to do it again. I was out to make an example of one in order to warn many."

BELONGING AND IDENTITY

"White prisoners think alike. They try to coexist with other gangs as long as they are not encroached upon. Most of the whites I've dealt with are druggies. This is their first priority. By ganging up together, they have a much greater chance of protecting their own supply and dealing to others. Some of the smarter ones try to get along with staff, thus avoiding unnecessary heat. Others are out to impress their peers, and they confront us. When they do, they lose. We bring whatever is necessary to take them down."

—Sergeant Bill Valentine

Hellraiser says that gangbangers feel special. "They belong to an elite group that not everyone can join. This makes us feel stronger and more powerful."

But as is the case with most young people who have yet to be totally entrenched in the gang life, Hellraiser feels that most white bangers want out. "They would like to have a better life and live another day without worry, just like everyone else."

I knew one 15-year-old white kid who started out as a tagger with several kids. The gang, which he led, was called Demonic Kings, and they spent a lot of their time tagging

"DK" all over Portland in large, stylistic writing. The tagging crew quickly evolved into a violent gang, clashing with fists and bullets with other gangs, especially Southeast Asians. The first time my partner and I arrested the kid, I asked if he had any tattoos. He responded by pulling up his T-shirt, revealing the letters DK, so large that they covered his entire upper body. I recall how his face glowed with pride over those letters and all that they meant to him.

POLICE

Hellraiser has no love for the police. "I feel cops don't give a shit about gangbangers and would like to see them all just kill themselves. I have heard many cops show little respect for my homies who have died, and I've heard them refer to them as scum and trash. Most cops have gotten used to gangbangers. They don't care about them . . . they just avoid the gang problem, thus saving their little asses.

"I have no love for any cop."

THE FUTURE

Hellraiser has mixed feelings about the future. "I feel that the gangbangers who live to be in their 20s or older have remorse for what they have done. You can only survive the street so long before it gets to you. Their attitude toward themselves may change, but with me, I feel I haven't changed because I've done what I had to do in order to survive."

Hellraiser concludes with this. "I feel society in general doesn't care that there are 13-year-old kids out there dying every night. Society just turns its back and tries to ignore the problem while making it even bigger."

My experience in working with white kids in gangs taught me that most, if not all of them, were delinquents to begin with, and when the gang phenomenon caught on, they just naturally progressed into it. I also found that the majority of them came from families where parenting skills were lacking or not there at all, and in some cases the parents were criminals and entangled in the justice system themselves.

I never saw a Dr. Spock book in white gangbangers' homes. What I did see were lives without structure and without a whole heck of a lot of caring from the parents. Therefore, it shouldn't come as a surprise that Hellraiser and thousands of others like him feel that society "doesn't care that there are 13-year-old kids dying out there every night."

The world these kids live in is small. It consists of their home, their neighborhood, and their school. When they have a lousy home life with uncaring parents, when they are having trouble in school from teachers and classmates, when their lives in the 'hood are full of danger from other gangbangers and "harassment" from the police, it's no wonder that they see society as uncaring.

CHAPTER 5

SOUTHEAST ASIAN GANGS

"Bui doi—life like dust."

A BRIEF HISTORY

Vietnamese, Laotian, Mien, Hmong, and Cambodian gangs represent the bulk of the Southeast Asian street gang problem in the United States. Vietnamese gangs first came to be in the late 1970s, followed by Laotian and Cambodian gangs in the early 1980s. The various gangs ranged in size from five to 200 members, and most were between the ages of 15 and 25. Of course, the older bangers were usually the leaders. Their crimes included robberies of private homes and businesses, car theft, and burglaries. Rarely were they involved in drive-by shootings back then.

Early Asian gangbangers didn't associate with each other on a continuous basis, nor did they have much loyalty to a particular gang. Unlike Hispanic and black gangs, Asian gangs began without the usual characteristics, such as tattoos, hand signs, or graffiti. They had no names for their gangs, nor were they organized or turf oriented. There were no female Asian gangs and only a few female Asian gang members.

But by 1985 Vietnamese gangs were on a roll, committing organized auto thefts, extortions, firearms violations, home-invasion robberies, witness intimidations, assaults, and murders. They mostly targeted their own communities with ruthless and vicious crimes, often traveling to various Vietnamese communities throughout the country to commit them. For example, a gang would commit a crime in Portland, Oregon, on a Monday, and by Friday we would get information that they were in Biloxi, Mississippi.

Laotian and Cambodian gangs were predatory. They became turf oriented, and their crimes were random property and person crimes—usually involving some form of robbery or burglary.

There are thousands of Southeast Asian gangbangers now, most of whom are in Vietnamese, Laotian, and Cambodian gangs. Some of the gangs, especially those consisting of young bangers, wear specific colors like the black gangs. Other gangs, however, especially those that have been around for a while, choose not to be as visible. Members now range in age from 13 to 35.

Southeast Asian gangs continue to terrorize and prey upon their communities through extortion, business and residential robberies, and drive-by shootings. As we will discuss in a moment, some of these crimes are extremely violent and brutal. The gangs have also increased their traveling patterns. We used to see them commute up and down the I-5 corridor on the West Coast and occasionally to the Midwest, but now they routinely travel from coast to coast committing their crimes.

Pamela Sowers, a writer and Southeast Asian gang observer, feels that the kids get into gangs for emotional reasons. "Southeast Asian gangbangers are looking for a home, a sense of community, and a sense of belonging. While their families may have tried to get them involved in community activities, gangbangers are aware of an emptiness at the heart of the family. Perhaps a dear family member died in the wars of Southeast Asia, or didn't make it to the states with the rest of the family. Perhaps early illness, a failure to thrive, or other physical problems made the child feel cut off from the people who would ordinarily be friends and classmates. There could have been a divorce, a car accident, or extreme poverty after generations of wealth. For whatever reason, the child grows into a stage that is commonly accepted in the broader American culture but is not in the Asian culture. He or she tries to rebel, to act out his or her separateness, and finds no place for that within the family structure. Any of these can make the gang structure very seductive.

"A banger stays in the gang because he is made to feel that he owes the gang. Additionally, this person is not likely to see all that it's taking away, like the chance for education, true respect in the community, and other intangibles."

When considering the difference between a person who willingly joins a gang and a person who, for whatever reason, is forced to join, Pamela Sowers says this. "Look at Chinese history. The forcibly enlisted soldier has always fought with a special vengeance when his stomach is full and he sees a chance of going home after the battle is over. If he sees no hope, he may fight even harder out of anger and humiliation. If the gang accepts him after he was forced to join, he may reason that it is because no one else will."

Many people feel a sense of mystery about Southeast Asian gangs and gangbangers, no doubt because of the language barrier and cultural differences. Here is how they think about various elements of gangbanging.

RESPECT

"No one would join a gang if he didn't think that he was going to gain."

—Pamela L. Sowers

Among other things, this Southeast Asian gang uses colors to get respect, such as the blue bandana they are displaying.

Gang Detective Stu Winn tells of a case he worked that sums up the concept of respect among Southeast Asian gangbangers. "I investigated an Asian gang homicide that happened in a coffee shop in which there was an Asian man who was from a powerful family and was well respected in the community. He was there with a younger friend.

"One day an Asian gangbanger, who had been giving the younger guy problems, shows up at the coffee shop. The older man comes to his friend's aid and says, 'Hey, leave my friend alone. I think of him as my younger brother. Don't screw with him anymore.'

"So, just saying those things to the gangbanger in a public place, talking down to him like that, enrages the banger. He sends one of his buddies out to the car to get a gun, and a second later he returns with it and gives it to the head banger. When the older man goes outside, the gangsters follow him out and the lead banger points the gun at him and starts threatening the man for the diss.

"The man says, 'OK, you think you are so big, then shoot. Go ahead and shoot.'

"The banger says, 'OK,' and shoots him in the face. When the man falls, the banger shoots him two more times in the back of the head. And when the man is completely prone, the banger empties his gun into him and then walks away.

"This whole incident was about respect and loss of face. The man even took the rounds, he got shot, because it would have been a loss of face for him to run away. So he just stood there straight on and said, 'Shoot me,' implying that he had no respect for the banger."

REPUTATION

"Reputation has to be one of the paramount motivations of most people on the social margins. There is much more emphasis on what others think of them than there is on the reality of the person in question."

—Pamela Sowers

The reputation of a Southeast Asian gang is known throughout the Asian community. The rep is based on the gang's crimes and acts of terror that its members carry out, mostly against other Asians who are afraid to tell the police.

Early on in Portland, racist skinheads held little respect for Southeast Asian gangbangers and often made catcalls at them on the street. But outside a teen club one night, the skinheads got a quick lesson. Four of them were standing on the corner when a Toyota with six Southeast Asian gangbangers passed by. The skinheads shouted out things like "gook," "Asian six-pack" and other derogatory names. The Asians continued down the street, rounded the block, and returned to the curb next to the skins. Shots exploded from the car, and one skinhead fell with a bullet in his groin, while the others scattered.

As you can imagine, racist skinheads held Southeast Asians in high regard after that and never harassed them again.

REVENGE

"Revenge has damned everything for some of the Southeast Asian gangsters."

—Pamela Sowers

Many Southeast Asian gangsters talk of a concept called "100-year revenge," meaning that if they get wronged in some fashion, they will seek revenge even if it takes 100 years. "If we can't get you," I have heard them say, "we will get your children, and if we can't get them, we will get their children. We will get revenge, even if it takes 100 years."

Pamela Sowers says that the 100-year revenge is mentioned frequently in Asian literature, such as *Outlaws of the Water Margin*, an ancient Chinese novel about gangsters, or "men of honor" as they were called many years ago—and as some still prefer to be addressed in Hong Kong. "The concept also shows up in some Asian movies," she says. "I know that today, in the case of a major transgression against a gang leader, his followers will try to kill or harm every family member of the transgressor. That has happened in Seattle with the Cambodian gangsters."

Detective Stu Winn said that he mostly hears about the 100-year concept from the older gangbangers as opposed to the younger ones. He related a story of how he first learned of it. "I had a Laotian informant who told me that years ago when he was in grammar school, another kid beat him up pretty severely. He decided to get revenge but not right away, because he wanted to wait until the timing was just right. Two years later he saw his opportunity when he noted that the kid rode the same bus every day. The Laotian kid went home, got a knife, and secreted it into his school books. He then watched the kid's movements for a couple of days, and when the timing was finally right, he attacked him on the bus and stabbed him multiple times. [The Laotian kid] was only in the fourth or fifth grade at the time."

The Laotian told Detective Winn that revenge was important in his culture and if it took 100 years to get it accomplished, then that's what he would do. What happens after 100 years? "The person is forgiven," the Laotian said. The bottom line is that whether it's one year or 100, Southeast gangbangers take their revenge very seriously. They also think in terms of redress—that is, they will strike out vigorously to make things right. This is especially true among some of the Vietnamese gangbangers.

This is my take on it based on what I have read. A few years ago, Vietnamese people lived in villages that were surrounded by wild vegetation and rice fields. There was never excess land, so if some people in the village accumulated wealth, they were looked upon as depriving the rest of the community of land while they got fat and others starved. While Vietnam no longer has a closed economic system, great wealth is still considered antisocial among many people, and a symbol of selfishness.

Vietnamese gangbangers feel—some more than others and some with greater levels of consciousness than others—that when they rob the wealthy they are correcting inequalities and equalizing the wealth (albeit into their personal pockets). They view their victims contemptuously, with anger and hatred, so that when they attack them they often do it with great violence. The victims, especially those who came to the United States in the mid-1970s, often express shock at the level of violence and the disrespect shown to the old people, pregnant mothers, and children. Although disrespect is considered culturally unacceptable, Southeast Asian gangbangers feel their actions are justified because they are seeking redress—that is, they are equalizing the wealth.

THEY THINK IN THE NOW

Keep in mind that many Southeast Asian gangbangers have no fear of going to prison. "Jail is just another place to be," they have responded when threatened by the police. Hearing them say such a thing shouldn't be too surprising when you consider what they have survived—war-torn homelands, an unbelievable voyage across the sea, and settlement in a country completely foreign to them. Compared with all that, how bad can jail be?

Since many of them don't fear jail, they don't hesitate to react violently when they have been wronged. I have seen many cases of Southeast Asian bangers who, because they got cut off in traffic, got caught prowling cars, or were in some way dissed on the school grounds, reacted by pulling out a gun and shooting the person or persons they felt were responsible for the slight.

This is what one Southeast Asian gangbanger, currently serving time in prison, says about acting in the now. "I know

Southeast Asian gangs often make a plan and implement it within minutes. Note the guns.

how easy it can be to take the wrong path. Take an example: You are out with your homeboys one night and a car cuts recklessly in front of you, and [the passengers] flip you off. That pisses you off, and you figure you'll take care of business right there. You pull out a gun, and your homeboys don't want to be left out, so they pull a piece too. By that time you're so worked up that you can't think straight, and maybe you're drunk or high too. So you and your homeboys start smokin' [shooting] at the other car. By the time you get back to your place, you're all paranoid and just fucked up—if you even make it back and don't get busted or killed.

"If you've been through this, you understand. My point is that when you're out with your homies, you never think of the consequences of your actions, so you gotta think about it now."

BELONGING AND IDENTITY

"A gangster's life is the life of a wanderer
A wanderer is a person with
No safe place to return to.
When you leave home you can never return:
To return is to be a coward.
To play is to play to the end.
We will live or die together.
We will share the good things,
And if there are bad things,
We will share those, too."

—Southeast Asian gangbanger poem

"Depending on the rules of the gang, you probably won't be able to get out of this mess until you're below ground permanently or the gang is abandoned. If the rules say you can get out whenever you want to, then you can; but some members will feel betrayed and go after that person or even his family.

"Unlike other ethnic gangs, like the black and Hispanic gangs, Asian gangs are pretty much part of the Asian community."

—an observer of Asian gang activity

"Fuck you, you stupid Mexican and black ass piece of shit! Think you all that or some shit! Fuck you! It's all about the Asians. Asian pride mutha fucker!"

—a Southeast Asian gangbanger

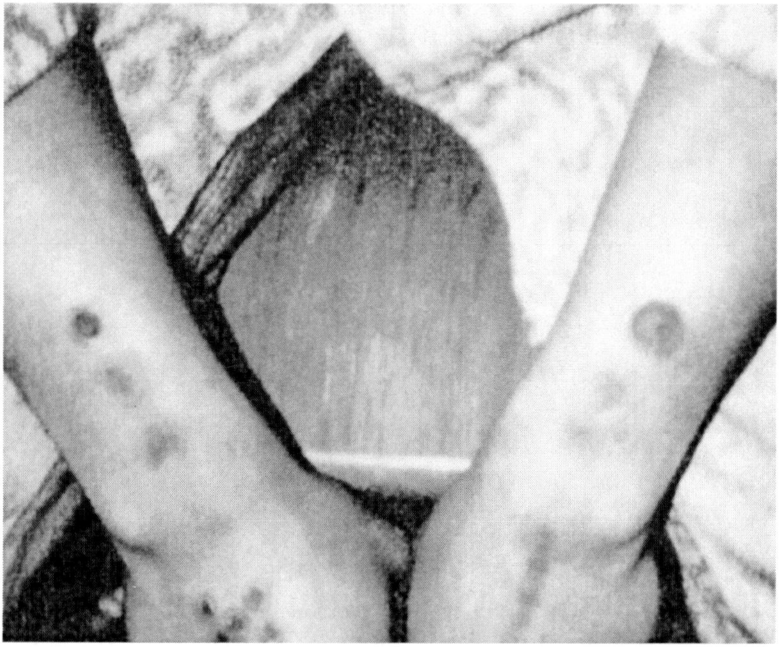

Southeast Asian bangers often apply cigarette burns to their hands and arms for various reasons, most commonly as a way of declaring that they are renegades and not part of the community.

"Fuck you, Busta! You be thinking youz really hard, rite? Gangs are smart too, you mutha fuck shit. We ain't like Blackass niggy's gangs or like White Honkies wannabee tough gangs, isn't that rite, loc? So you can say allllllll this fuckin shit, or you could just respect my pride in my gang. Kauz this is a thang for life, and ain't no fucking gayass chinky nerd gonna tell me shit! You got that, you mutha fuck shit!"

—from a Southeast Asian gangbanger's letter

Note, that by using terminology such as "youz really hard, rite?," "Honkies," "mutha," and "thang," that he is emulating black-style gangs. Since he replaces the letter "c" with a "k" in "kauz" he is probably related to the Bloods.

Southeast Asian gangs often emulate black and Hispanic gangs in their affectations, such as their use of hand signals.

Pamela Sowers talks about the importance of symbols to the Asian gangbanger's sense of belonging. "Symbols, such as tattoos, gang clothing, hand signs, are significant. Why does the military do the same thing? Each of these items in their turn has provided a sense of identity for the gang. They create an image in the minds of victims and bystanders, and they surely help recruiting. Would you join my gang if I said, 'Yeah, we're cool. We listen to Mantovani and chew gum.'? You'd be a heck of a lot more interested if I say, 'To get in, you've gotta have this cool python tattoo, a leather jacket, and wear only red shirts. Of course, you gotta suffer, to show you are a man.

"The English Restoration motto of 'Live fast, die young, leave a good-looking corpse' would be embraced by them if they ever sat through that kind of literature class. They see no future beyond next week, or perhaps their next birthday, so they see no reason to plan, save, or create anything lasting. As a result, if they have anything at all, it's all on the surface—car, clothes, guns, and girls. So often, juvenile gangsters are so far behind the eight-ball, they can't get any of the things that count for status beyond their colors and their weapons. Those are the ones who really scare me—they have nothing left to lose."

Two Faces

Some observers say that Southeast Asian gangbangers have two faces: one for the public, in particular their dealings with the Americans, and one for private, when they're dealing with their fellow gangbangers. They are not always successful with this, which causes confusion between the two worlds. This can lead to inconsistencies in their behavior, which often causes even more confusion and many misunderstandings within the gang and their families. With their peers, they may come across as too Americanized, and with their American contacts, they may be criticized for being too Asian.

Stress and alienation are serious problems among the so-called second-wave refugees. They have to struggle to get along in the new American world, while at the same time they must struggle to continue their existence in their Asian culture.

Then there are the children of the first-wave families, those who arrived in the 1970s, who are too young to have experienced the horrors of the wars in Southeast Asia. Since their families have money, they have enjoyed material pleasures. Nonetheless, they experience confusion and frustration because they get accused of being too American by their parents, who want them to be more Asian. But when they put on their Asian face, they can't get along at school where there are mostly non-Asian students.

Young first- and second-wave immigrants face a constant struggle to fit into both worlds. Some of those who lose the struggle will give up trying. When that happens and they no longer live a double life, the gang (and all that it has to offer) becomes a place of comfort in their confused life.

Police investigators also see two faces when interviewing Southeast Asian gangbangers. They put on a "game face" when talking with the police, especially when they've had time to prepare for the interview. Detectives say the bangers con them, use mind games, and appear to be helping them, though they're really not. But when a banger doesn't have time to prepare, the police often see a different face. For example, when detectives go to a gangbanger's home unannounced, they often find a different face at the door, one that is unpleasant and uncooperative.

Tattoos

Southeast Asian gangbangers may or may not be tattooed. Asians with dragons and swastika-like symbols may not necessarily be gang involved, though these symbols are definitely found on bangers. Often Southeast Asians tattoo themselves with ink, so it can be easily removed. Here are a few of the tattoos that indicate how they think.

- The words "Asian pride."
- Various animal that symbolize good luck and power: dragons (the most common), tigers, panthers, and cobras.
- Swastika, a Buddhist symbol.
- Gang names and their individual street monikers (these may be written in English or their native language).

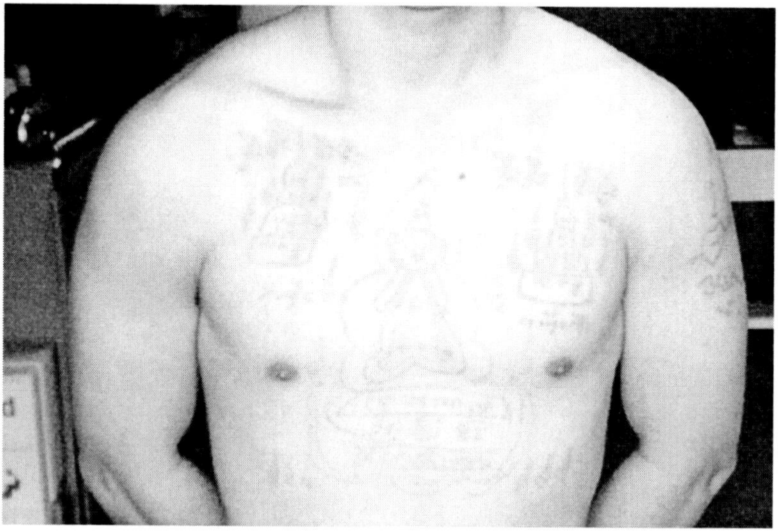

Some Southeast Asian bangers mark their bodies with ink as well as permanent tattooing. Note: Dragons and swastikas have may meanings and do not always indicate gang involvement.

- Four, sometimes five, letter "Ts, often seen on ex-cons These letters state to all what they consider important: *tinh* (love), *tu* (prison), *tien* (money), *toi* (crime), *thu* (revenge, which is not always present).

VIOLENCE

"Most Asian gangbangers who have a single burn mark on, say, their arm (usually a cigarette burn) have it as a symbol of their willingness to do criminal activity."

—a gang observer

"Bangers are fascinated with weapons and will generally be armed with the best available. They prefer high-capacity handguns, semiautomatic and automatic weapons."

—a gang observer

Weapons and ammo taken in a search warrant of a Southeast Asian gang house.

"Don't underestimate Asian gangbangers because of their size."

—a gang observer

Detective Stu Winn says that at least some of their approach to violence can be related to their religion. "They come here to the United States with Buddhist values, many of which are really good, but they also have some things built into their psyches that make the value of life different from the way Caucasians see it. So, when they stand in front of a house and spray it with 75 rounds from an assault rifle and there is a danger that the occupants will shoot back, they are thinking that their time here is fixed anyway, and they are going to a better place. They see themselves as just a small cog in this big machine. They have a different view of destiny.

"A lot of the gangbangers I talk with say there is not a lot they can do to control death. 'If it's your time, it's your time,' they say. So, if they go up against another gang or fight anoth-

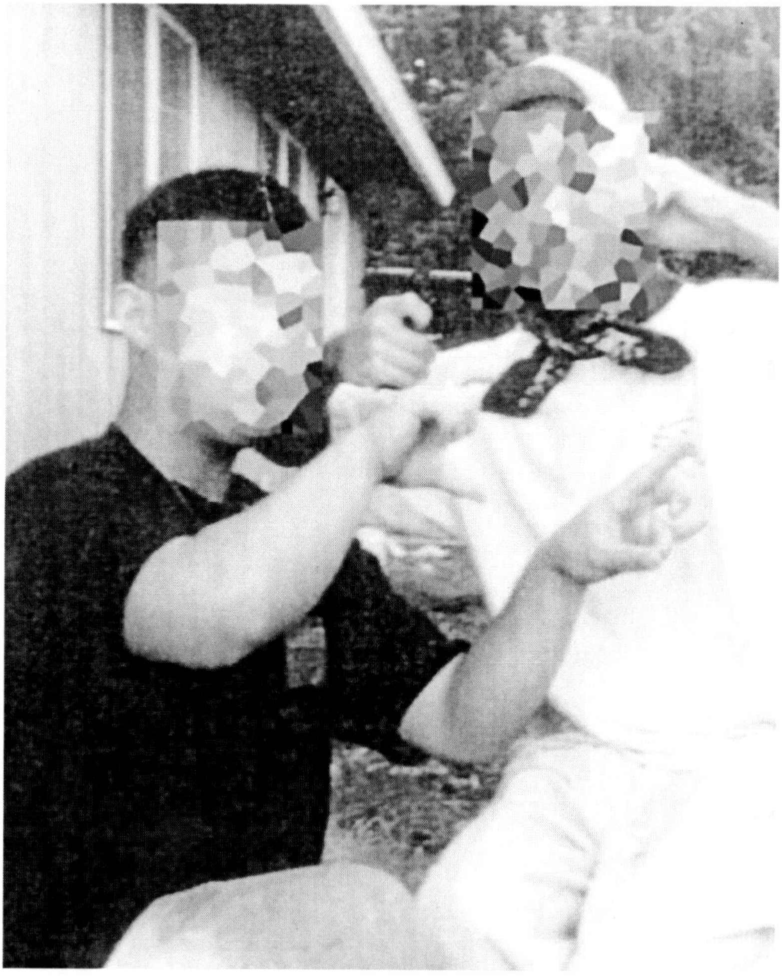

"Don't underestimate Asian gangbangers because of their size," warn gang experts and law enforcement personnel.

er gangbanger and if it's their time to go, well, then it's their time to go. If we pick up a gun to go and do a crime, we may think that we'd better be careful or we'll get killed. But the bangers say, 'There is nothing I can do because someone else

Southeast Asian bangers sprayed this house, killing a man inside. This picture shows where detectives marked 19 of the hits, but there were more.

rolled the dice on that, and I can't get it changed. It's destiny.'

"They think in terms of 'if it's Mr. Nguyen's time to die, then he dies. If he gets hit when I'm shooting at his house with my AK-47, and he gets killed, then it must have just been his time to die, even though he wasn't my intended target. It's not even my fault. It's simply Mr. Nguyen's destiny, and I am a small part of it. And if Mr. Nguyen grabs his gun and drills me first, then it must be my destiny to die now, and there is nothing I can do about that either.'"

When Southeast Asian gangbangers do a shooting for whatever reason, there is almost always going to be a retaliation shooting. The communities know that it's going to happen, and the parents of the gangbangers know that it's going to happen, often sleeping on the floor in the back of the house until the shooting goes down. Southeast Asian bangers, like a lot of young people in gangs, often act spontaneously. But there are also occasions when they plan their shootings. Detective Winn says, "At times, they'll make a master plan for a hit, maybe not like a military operation or anything to that extent, but they will plan it out."

Stu Winn is seeing more of the veteran gangbangers doing the shootings while the young ones stay in the car. These are old-time bangers who have nothing to prove but simply want to do the shooting. He says that it's as if they want to ensure that it goes down right.

Pamela Sowers see the violence as senseless. "The drive-bys I've been exposed to were based on such stupidity as racism, failure to get a date with a girl, a drug turf war, and a desire for status. They carry out some of their shootings with total disregard for innocents because they want to belong to the group and serve the interests of the people in the group they most admire. They do it for revenge, respect, and, in some cases, to cut a romantic or heroic figure.

"Southeast Asian gangbangers are much more fatalistic than other criminals. They are afraid of not fitting into American society, and they see themselves as never having what they see in the materialistic society around them. When things are so emphasized, and you don't have the things and there is no way of getting them, what does that do to optimism?"

Other authorities on Southeast Asian gangbangers, who will remain anonymous to protect them from accusations of being racist, say that the Cambodian, Lao, and Thai gangs carry out the most violent shootings. They do the spray-bys where everything, and sometimes everyone, gets shot.

"The Cambodians seem like the most lawless of the people I deal with," one observer noted. "They had all the horrific experiences trying to leave their country, and they don't follow many of the rules of conduct that are more familiar to me in the Chinese and Vietnamese cultures." Police investigators and gang observers say that even though Vietnamese gangbangers can be ruthless, their violence is not quite the same as that of the Cambodians. Rather than doing spray-by shootings, their approach is to simply walk up behind their target and shoot the person in the back of the head.

As mentioned a moment ago, at times there seems to be a

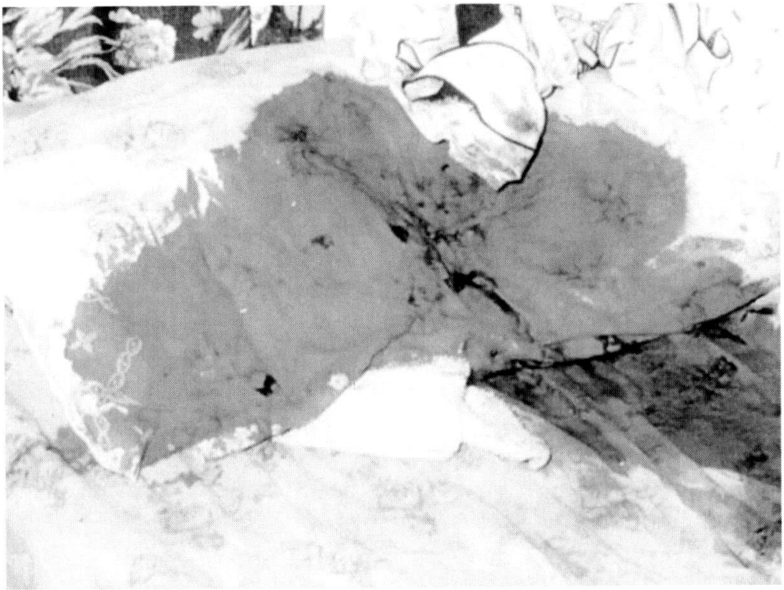

The bloody aftermath of a drive-by shooting by a Southeast Asian gang that killed a man sleeping in bed.

sense of dramatic flair to the actions of Southeast Asian gangbangers, a sense of acting as a romantic figure. All ethnic gangs try to display a certain look and style in their dress and actions, but there is something extra in the way that Southeast Asian bangers do it. For example, their cars are often easy to spot because of the extras that have been added to them, such as skirts, chrome, tinted windows, and lowered frames. Their dress is straight out of fashion catalogs, their sunglasses are chosen to emphasize "the look," and their strut and posturing are designed to show it off.

As if shooting at people isn't dramatic enough, they often do it with a flash straight out of a B-grade movie. For example, several of them with shaved heads and dressed in long overcoats and sunglasses will walk into an Asian restaurant and stand menacingly by the door as the restaurant occupants stare at them in horror. Then, with a move that strikes terror into the chests of the restaurant occupants, one or more of the gangbangers will pull back the flap of their overcoats, lift up automatic weapons that they had been holding alongside their legs, and spray the bar, tables, and occupants.

"The Vietnamese gangbangers definitely have a romantic view about their firepower," Detective Stu Winn says. "They have nice guns—.40 calibers, stainless steels, Smith and Wessons—while the other Asian gangs often have lower quality. The males love the fancy cars and love to be seen in the night clubs with beautiful women. And Asian women and some white women definitely like them. The bangers may be outcasts in their community and seen as bringing dishonor and shame to their families, but in the minds of the gangbangers, their gang lives and all their criminal activities make them heroes."

Southeast Asian gangbangers commonly treat their victims with disdain, beating the elderly, raping females, and abusing young children. They target Asians more than non-Asians, because they know that Southeast Asians usually don't trust the police or understand how the justice system works. Therefore, the crimes go unreported.

On the other hand, Detective Stu Winn says that Southeast Asian bangers have discovered that they can't always intimidate non-Asians as easily as they do members of their own race. "Whenever they've tried to intimidate people like Big Bill down at Bill's Steakhouse, they've found themselves on the receiving end of Big Bill's baseball bat. Asian victims, though, are more easily intimidated, and there is always a huge victim pool."

POLICE

Detective Stu Winn says there is a marked difference between interviewing Asian gangbangers and other gang members. "When I investigate crimes with black gangbangers, there is usually a confrontational atmosphere, and they lie to me a lot. This is almost instinctual with them. However, the Asian bangers are more cooperative, as if they are thinking, 'The police are here, I'm here. I think we can work this out. I think we can get along.' They'll make an effort to cooperate, even when they're a suspect in a case, because they believe they will get further with you. I think some of this comes from their old culture from their homeland, that there is a real value placed on harmony, even if it's surface harmony."

Many of them are fascinated with the fact that cops get to carry guns. Winn says that they like to talk shop with cops about their weapons. "They see the police as people living in their world while carrying a gun, and they see that as cool. They don't deal with the police with the same disdain that other gangs do. They will lie to you and lead you on all kinds of wild goose chases, but there is a different feeling in the relationship."

One big difference that Winn sees is that many Southeast Asian gangbangers have no remorse for their crimes, no matter how horrific. "With other ethnic gang members and non-gang-involved criminals, I try to play on their remorse for the hurt they have caused. But I find with Southeast Asian bangers, they don't have it. They laugh at my attempts to make them feel bad for what they have done, especially when their crimes involve revenge or redress."

In Pamela Sowers' experience, Southeast Asian gangbangers see the police as being outside of their communities. "They might respect some officers, but they see the police mostly as someone to test, someone who is outside the arguments they have between the gangs and the gang factions. Officers are rarely, if ever, seen as a part of the community the gangbangers are living in. So officers are not perceived as having a role in the turf and market-share problems confronting many gangs. I have found that a few gangsters find the general run of police officer amusing."

CHAPTER 6

FACT AND FICTION ABOUT YOUTH GANGS

Fiction: Gangbangers rarely go to school.

Fact: Although parents and school officials often deny that there are gangs in their schools, an overwhelming majority of gangbangers want to stay in school because they can congregate and discuss their activities, work on their reputations, flaunt their regalia, show their strength, protect their members, intimidate others, recruit members, and sometimes carry out violent acts. Some gangbangers—in particular Southeast Asians and, increasingly, Hispanics—believe in the importance of getting an education.

Fiction: Gangbangers come from families at the low end of the socioeconomic strata of society.

Fact: That may have been true to some extent in the early years of gangs, but today's gangbangers represent all levels of society. Police officers report that kids from wealthy neighborhoods and families now commute to rundown, gang-infested neighborhoods to hang out and participate in gang activity.

Fiction: Gang graffiti are just another kind of vandalism.

Fact: It is vandalism, but because graffiti frequently lead to violence they also send a message of fear. Gangs use graffiti to mark their territory, advertise their gang's status, declare their allegiance to the gang, and threaten rivals. Much violence has occurred over the simple act of marking symbols on a wall, especially when rivals retaliate. And all people on the street or in their homes are subject to being injured when bullets begin flying.

Fiction: Only males join gangs.

Fact: Females are increasingly involved in the activities of all gangs. They often carry the weapons and drugs, do drive-by shootings, instigate acts of violence, participate in fights, and in some gangs act as leaders. Gang experts say that females have the same mental processes regarding gang activity as do the males. Many give birth to babies with the intent of raising them to be future gangbangers. One female skinhead told me, "I want six Aryan children, and I'm going to give them all German names."

Fiction: Gangs are only an inner-city problem.

Fact: Gangbangers are spreading like a brush fire. It's common now for urban, drug-dealing gangs to migrate to smaller cities and rural and suburban areas in search of fresh drug markets, less competition, and higher profits. With the media attention on gangs, especially the glamorization of gangs in movies, television dramas, music videos, and clothing styles, more and more young, impressionable people throughout the country are adopting gang lifestyles and activities.

Fiction: Gangs are made up of only black and Hispanic young people.

Fact: As we have seen in this book, that common belief is obviously untrue, though movies and television programs would make it seem so. The reality is that gang membership crosses all racial, ethnic, social, and economic lines. And now there are growing numbers of white youths throughout the country who are forming their own gangs (not just skinheads) or joining the ranks of ethnic gangs, emulating their dress and unique gang speak.

Fiction: Kids join gangs because their parents don't care what they do.

Fact: Most parents of gangbangers care about their children (though there are some who clearly don't). The problem is that many of the young bangers come from dysfunctional families where there are poverty, unemployment, lack of education, and weak or nonexistent family support systems, and where the adults don't speak English or understand American customs and culture. As a result, many parents are unable to resolve problems with their children before they become crises. Single parents often feel frustrated and alone because they have little or no emotional and psychological support when their children become involved in gangs.

Fiction: Young people join gangs to make big money because they don't want jobs paying only minimum wage.

Fact: Not everyone joins a gang to make money. For some, gang membership is a matter of survival in their neighborhood; for others it is simply to follow in the footsteps of older brothers, sisters, or other relatives. Some join because they are looking for a strong support system, because they lack one in their family or community. Those who do get involved to make money do so because they feel that jobs are not available to them or because they lack the skills necessary to apply for a job.

Fiction: All gangs are a cohesive group with a single leader.

Fact: This is a common fallacy perpetuated by Hollywood movies, which often depict a gang leader standing before a group of gangbangers and barking out orders. The truth is that most gangs are loosely knit and either have no leadership or have several members who fill leadership roles. The leadership may change daily, since most active gang members are in and out of the justice system, not to mention their high mortality rate. Keep in mind, though, that gangbangers are antiauthority and have problems taking orders from anyone.

Fiction: One way to cure the gang problem is to lock gang members away.

Fact: Incarceration of hard-core gang members does get them off the street and prevent them from hurting others, but it has not been proven to be effective for getting people out of gangs. Prisons often serve as "institutions of higher learning" for ongoing gang-related crime. Prisoners are forced to take sides with one gang or another simply for protection and survival. Research suggests that the most effective response to gang problems includes prevention, intervention, and suppression strategies.

Fiction: Gang violence is directed only at other gangs.

Fact: Other gangbangers are the most frequent victims of gangbangers' violence, but many innocent bystanders get hurt, too. With the tendency of gangs to use high-tech weapons to spray bullets, many rounds miss their intended targets and keep right on traveling until they are stopped by other people. Additionally, there are some gangs, particularly, racist skinheads and Southeast Asians, that target innocent people.

Fiction: Gangbangers are *just* kids acting out.

Fact: Yes, most of them are just kids and they are definitely acting out, but saying it this way is too simplistic and naive. It is often heard from people denying that street gangs are in their community. Keep in mind that some of these kids stand over 6 feet tall and carry more than 200 pounds of institution-developed muscle. Those who are shorter and weigh less appear much larger when they pull a MAC 10 from under an oversized coat and point it at a victim's face. The bottom line is that these kids are dangerous because all of them have access to lethal weapons and some won't hesitate to use them.

Fiction: All gangbangers can be saved.

Fact: According to everyone interviewed in this book, most kids want out of the gang life. When given love, attention, education, and an opportunity to develop self-esteem, it has been found that most will leave the lifestyle. Others, though, must reach an age of maturity, usually their early 20s, and graduate from gangs on their own. There are some who won't give up their gang membership but will move into other areas of criminality, usually the drug business.

John Miller, a supervisor in the Department of Juvenile and Adult Community Justice, illustrates the scale of gang involvement. Spreading his arms wide, he states, "This is the population of kids in our country." He then holds his right thumb and index finger about four inches apart: "The number of kids involved in gangs make up this much of the total population of young people." Narrowing his thumb and index finger to about 1/4-inch apart, he says, "This is how many bangers are absolutely hard-core and probably beyond saving."

Fiction: Gangs are made up of the same ethnic or racial group.

Fact: Today, the only gangs that claim to be 100 percent racially or ethnically pure are racist skinheads. To their chagrin, however, even they occasionally discover that one of their own is Jewish or of some other ethnicity. Antiracist skinheads, however, are often populated with blacks, Asians, and

Hispanics. So-called black gangs are no longer all black, Hispanic gangs are more and more mixed with whites and blacks, and many Southeast Asian gangs are now a mix of Vietnamese, Cambodian, Laotian, Hmong, and even whites.

Fiction: Kids who get involved in gangs are trying to fulfill emotional needs that are not met in their dysfunctional families.

Fact: This describes the home environment of most gangbangers. However, as a result of movies, music videos, and clothing that glamorize gang life and gangbangers, more and more young people from solid homes are seeking the excitement of gangbanging.

Fiction: Gangbangers love the attention they get.

Fact: Some do, and some don't. Some collect their press clippings and videotape the five o'clock news segment that showcases their crimes. Others don't want it at all because they want to carry out their activities anonymously.

Fiction: Racist skinheads attack only minorities.

Fact: Once again Hollywood has misled people. Racist and neo-Nazi skinheads actually attack white people much more than they attack minorities. They attack whites who disagree with their philosophy and beliefs, or whites they perceive to be homosexual, Jewish, and sympathizers of various minorities.

Fiction: "Gangsta rap" and other kinds of gang music is OK. It's just music.

Fact: Tom Metzger, 60-year-old founder of White Aryan Resistance (WAR), realized years ago that the best way to get his hate-filled, racist views across to skinheads was through music. Music is a big part of young people's lives; they listen to it intently, and they are moved by the words. The popularity of gangsta rap, a form of hip-hop music that glorifies inner-city gang life, has grown rapidly in the past few years. Gangsta rap artists like Snoop Doggy Dogg (who was charged as an accessory to murder) and Tupac Shakur (who was killed in a drive-by shooting in Los Angeles) are idolized by young teens who long to be like these tough, fearsome gangsters. In fact, Shakur's death made him a martyr, and he is deified by millions of teens who see him as a symbol of rebellion against the system.

Fiction: A wanna-be is a kid pretending to be a gangbanger.

Fact: I know that the concept of wanna-bes is discussed throughout this book, but it's so important that I want to reiterate it here. Too often the word is used by people who are in denial or want to play down a young person's involvement. The fact is, if a kid thinks he's a Crip, an 18th Street, or a Viet Boy, then he is. Just because he hasn't been beaten into a gang yet doesn't make him any less dangerous. Even full-fledged gangbangers recognize that wanna-bes are extremely dangerous, even more dangerous than the regulars. "The real dangerous ones are the wanna-bes," one banger told me. They want to be a banger in the worst way, and they will often do anything to prove that they have what it takes.

Fiction: Gang members don't live in my neighborhood.

Fact: How do you know? Gangbangers are starting to change the way they dress to avoid detection by law enforcement. Although they used to brag about being in a gang, more and more are denying their membership. Some gangbangers do well in school, and since they aren't wearing the usual gang attire, you would never guess they are involved.

Fiction: Various types of outreach programs designed to get kids out of gangs have been tremendously helpful.

Fact: Most of the people I interviewed, even those in outreach programs, question the value of these programs. The gangbangers I spoke with say the programs are good for amusement only and that the bangers laugh behind the workers' backs. One observer did note that they are probably of value to young people who are less committed and to those who are easily distracted by programs that are more attractive than the gang culture.

Fiction: My children aren't in gangs.

Fact: Maybe not, but if you allow them to dress like gangbangers, they will be at risk from real ones. When the real bangers notice that your kids are dressing the part, they may be attacked because they're seen as a threat, even though they don't belong to a gang. Nongang members have been killed because of the way they dress.

Fiction: Gangs just affect other gangs.

Fact: Gangs affect all of us. The following are just a few of the ways:

- They increase crime in the community.
- They increase the cost for police and city services.
- They increase the burden on the social service systems and emergency and medical systems.
- They increase the costs of security services for businesses and schools.
- They damage the image of a city.
- They influence business recruitment and the overall city economic development.
- They increase the likelihood of innocent people getting hurt.
- They cause trauma, grief, confusion, and depression over injury and death from gang violence.
- They damage personal property through acts of vandalism.
- They increase fear.

Fiction: Gang activity only takes place in the 'hood.

Fact: Gangs are everywhere, including the following locations:

- High school, middle school, grade school
- Movie theaters, arcades
- Parks and recreation centers
- Shopping centers
- Apartment and multidwelling complexes
- Grocery and convenience stores
- Public transportation
- Hospital waiting rooms and emergency rooms

CONCLUSION

NOW WHAT?

As I noted at the beginning of this book, gangs are not going away any time soon. In a short span they have spread to every part of the country: big cities, little towns, and rural areas. The question of "now what?" is as easy to ask as it is difficult to answer.

Many ideas have been implemented—some have worked, and some haven't. Some people feel that we must intercept the kids when they are very young and at risk. Yes, that will work. Other people think we should catch them after they commit a crime and put them away in the joint for a long time. Yes, that works, too. Most efforts work to some degree, but nothing is 100-percent effective because there is no one solution. The problem is just too complex and big.

Maybe it's time to examine the problem from a different perspective. Perhaps some of the solutions are in the minds of the gangbangers. Rather than standing on the outside and throwing "remedies" at them, let's look inside at how they think. Maybe, just maybe, the answers have been there all along.

GLOSSARY

If you have children, you know difficult it is to keep up with their latest slang words. Well, it's even harder to stay abreast of gang slang. It changes quickly, and much of it is regional, meaning that words and expressions that are fashionable in Chicago may or may not be used in California, and vice versa.

There are some words and expressions, however, that have remained popular over the years. I have listed some of them here to give you a sense of how gangbangers communicate and how they think.

Free tip: unless you are gangbanger, don't try to use these words in an attempt to relate to gang members. Not only will you sound silly, but they will laugh at you behind your back—and sometimes right to your face.

BLACK GANGS

5-0: Police.
187: Murder (California penal code).
911: Police.
A.K.: AK-47 rifle.
A.R.: AR-15 rifle.
A.K./Uzi: Semiautomatic weapon.
all that: In possession of all good qualities.
B.K.: Initials meaning *Blood killer*; used by Crip gangs to threaten rival Blood gangs.
B.K.A.: Blood killer always.

Black Gangster Disciple: A Chicago-based street gang founded in the late 1960s or early 1970s.
Blood: A member of a LA gang whose color is red.
blob/slob: Crips' derogatory term for a Blood.
booty: Not good; lacking; bottom, ass, or getting a piece of ass.
bumper kit: A girl's butt.
bumping titties: Fighting.
busted/popped a cap: Shot at something.
banging: Doing gang activity.
crib: A person's home, an inmate's cell, room.
Crip: A member of an L.A. gang whose color is blue; Blue down L.A. based gang nation.
crumbs: Tiny pieces of rock cocaine.
cuzz: Friendly term used by Crips when referring to other Crips.
down (being down for something): Favoring something; thinking the same way.
deuce & deuce or double deuce: A .22-caliber weapon.
diss: Disrespect.
down for the hood: Loyal to the neighborhood.
flying your color: Wearing the colors of your gang.
Folk: Chicago-based gang nation
gage: shotgun.
gangbanger: an active gang member.
gat: Gun.
homeboy or homegirl: Gang member.
holmes: A person from a neighborhood. Also means homeboy and homey.
homey, homeboy: Close friend.
hood: Neighborhood.
jump in: Gang initiation.
nut up: Angry.
O.G.: Original gang member.
packing: Gang member with a gun.

People/People Nation: A coalition of Midwestern including the Vice Lords and affiliate groups th formed an organized criminal group of gangs/se
R.I.P.: "Rest in Peace." Often seen in graffiti and is a cation of pending violence or violence that has a occurred.
rag: Handkerchief in gang's color.
rag: Color of a gang.
shooter: A gang member who uses a gun.
set: Neighborhood gangs; another term used for a gan criminal street gang members. Most sets are loyal to fall under a larger umbrella gang, such as the Bloods Crips, Folks, or People.
shank: Prison term for homemade knife.
slob: Crip's word for Blood gang member.
tagger: Someone who uses graffiti.
tray-eight: .38-caliber weapon.
What it B like?: Blood greeting.
What it C like?: Crip greeting.

HISPANIC GANGS

13 or XIII or X3 or Trece: Thirteenth letter in the alphabet (M), which symbolizes or identifies gang affiliation of Mexican heritage. Also may refer to allegiance to Southern California gangs.
14 or XIV or X4: Fourteenth letter of the alphabet (N), which refers to allegiance to Northern California.
barrio: Neighborhood.
chingate: Fuck yourself.
chiva: Heroin.
chivero: Heroin addict.
chola: Girl involved in gang activity.
cholo: Boy involved in gang activity.
chota: Police.

homies: Fellow gang members.
homeboy: Southeast Asian who avoids trouble; a youth who stays home.
mutha fuck: Mutha fucker.
party lights: A police car's overhead lights.
play: Committing a crime.
school boy: A Southeast Asian who attends school.

SKINHEAD GANGS

88: Short for "Heil Hitler." Derived from the fact that the letter H is the eighth letter of the alphabet. Racist and Nazi skins often say "88" as a form of greeting, and they scrawl it on any- and everything as a way to pass on their message.
bonehead: Term used by antiracists to describe a racist skinhead.
boot party: This is a term derived from the heavy boots that are used to beat a victim senseless. A boot party always involves several skinheads against one victim.
braces: Suspenders. According to some sources, their color no longer has significance, although at one time, white and red were worn by racist skinheads, and green was worn by SHARPs. Since new people join the ranks every day, it's possible that colors are still significant in some areas of the country.
brother, comrade: A fellow skinhead.
Doc Martens: A style of boot, usually black or oxblood with multiple eyelets. To skinheads, the significance of the boots is just as great as colors are to black gangs. The boots symbolize who they are and what they believe. It's not uncommon for them to stick their boots toward the camera when they are having their picture taken.
flight [jacket]: Their flight jackets—which can be gray, green, black, or brown—are probably second in significance to

the Doc Martens. The skins adorn them with pen scrawls and patches that denote their philosophy and politics. So important is the flight jacket that they will wear it on scorching-hot days.

kick ass: A not too creative term meaning to beat someone up.

salute: This is the straight-arm salute that racist skinheads snap out, the same salute used by Hitler's Nazis. They do it as a way to greet each other, show unity, and taunt rivals.

shaved for battle: This refers to the skinhead's bald head and means he is ready to fight for his beliefs.

swastika: For racist skinheads, the symbol denotes their belief in their racial superiority and their fascination with everything Nazi Germany stood for.

ABOUT THE AUTHOR

Loren W. Christensen retired recently after 29 years in law enforcement. He served with the military police in Vietnam and stateside and as an officer with the Portland Police Bureau in Oregon. While with the Portland Police Bureau, Loren worked a variety of jobs, including street patrol, defensive tactics instructor, dignitary protection, and as a specialist in skinhead street gangs with the Gang Enforcement Team.

Today, Loren is a full-time writer, martial arts teacher, and private consultant on personal security matters for businesses. He continues to monitor the gang situation in this country and writes about it for various magazines. Loren's book *Skinhead Street Gangs*, published by Paladin Press, has been used as a reference during the production of television documentaries and motion pictures.

Loren Christensen's Internet site is http://www.aracnet.com/~lwc123/.